Writing History

A Guide for Students

CANADIAN EDITION

William Kelleher Storey
&
Towser Jones

OXFORD
UNIVERSITY PRESS

1904 ❦ 2004

100 YEARS OF
CANADIAN PUBLISHING

OXFORD
UNIVERSITY PRESS

70 Wynford Drive, Don Mills, Ontario M3C 1J9
www.oup.com/ca

Oxford University Press is a department of the University of Oxford.
It furthers the University's objective of excellence in research, scholarship,
and education by publishing worldwide in

Oxford New York
Auckland Bangkok Buenos Aires Cape Town Chennai
Dar es Salaam Delhi Hong Kong Istanbul Karachi Kolkata
Kuala Lumpur Madrid Melbourne Mexico City Mumbai Nairobi
São Paulo Shanghai Taipei Tokyo Toronto

Oxford is a trade mark of Oxford University Press
in the UK and in certain other countries

Published in Canada
by Oxford University Press

Copyright © Oxford University Press Canada 2004

The moral rights of the author have been asserted

Database right Oxford University Press (maker)

First published 2004

National Library of Canada Cataloguing in Publication Data

Storey, William Kelleher
Writing history : a guide for students / William Kelleher Storey,
Towser Jones. – 1st Canadian ed.

Includes index.
ISBN 0-19-541998-7

1. History—Research. 2. History—Research—Canada. 3. Academic
writing. 4. Historiography. 5. Historiography—Canada. I. Jones, Towser II. Title.

D16.S76 2004   907'.2   C2003-907331-9

Cover design: Brett J. Miller
Cover image: Stephen Johnson / Getty Images

1 2 3 4 - 07 06 05 04
This book is printed on permanent (acid-free) paper ∞.
Printed in Canada

⊰ Contents ⊱

⊰ Preface ⊱

This book introduces the challenges of writing history. It contains technical advice, but it is more than just a style manual; it shows how historians select topics, analyze sources, and build arguments. In short, it is a practical guide for beginning historians.

Writing History had its origins in the Harvard Writing Project, a collaborative effort between Harvard's Expository Writing Program and other departments to improve undergraduate writing. Between 1995 and 1997, while I was teaching writing courses at Harvard, my chair, Nancy Sommers, put me in contact with professors from the History Department and the History of Science Department who were reforming the ways in which their departments taught writing. As I worked with faculty members, especially with Mark Kishlansky and Mark Madison, it became clear that both students and teachers would benefit from a short guide. I wrote two booklets for Harvard, and as I circulated drafts to friends and colleagues at other universities, I began to realize that there was a wide demand for a guide to writing history.

While working on the first edition, published in 1999, I benefited from the advice, comments, and criticism of Tony English, Jim Goodman, Gordon Harvey, Maura Henry, Bill Kirby, Mark Kishlansky, Susan Lively, Mark Madison, Everett Mendelsohn, Nancy Sommers, Mary Terrall, and Jon Zimmerman. Since that time, I have been teaching with the book at Millsaps College, where my students and colleagues have made a number of suggestions for improvement. The second edition now contains important revisions, including expanded sections on plagiarism, interviewing, topic selection, and the use of the Internet in historical research. In preparing the second edition, I am grateful to several anonymous reviewers, as well as to Jan Beatty, Christine Lutz, Ellen Stroud, and once again, Mark Kishlansky, for helpful suggestions.

One thing has not changed since the first edition. I still wish to acknowledge the six people who have done the most to encourage me to learn how to write history. They are my teachers, Philip Curtin, Robin Kilson, and Scotty Royce; my parents, Bill and Mary Storey; and my wife, Joanna Miller Storey.

Preface to the Canadian Edition

Since the American version of this book, now in its second edition, is so strong, why would we need a specifically Canadian one? Are we Canadians not accustomed to reading texts from elsewhere, and are we not frequently exhorted to see Canada as part of a wider, world culture?

In seeing the world, however, we do not want to overlook Canada. Therefore it is important that students are aware of Canadian context, and of the uniquely Canadian experience—including Canadian history.

Preparing the Canadian edition of William Kelleher Storey's fine book has been a pleasure. I have left intact his tone (chatty) and organization (practical) and tried to preserve the flavour of his work. I have retained much of Storey's text and his examples drawn from world history. My changes and additions are designed to provide examples that will have meaning especially for Canadian students. I also hope to introduce students to at least a small sample of excellent Canadian scholars, and to direct them to some specifically Canadian research materials.

Like most authors, I have debts to honour. I am happy to acknowledge William Kelleher Storey for creating such a fine text. Laura Macleod of Oxford University Press has been an encouraging and patient editor. I am grateful to the anonymous reviewer who saved me from some errors and made insightful suggestions. My friend, colleague and mentor, Robert Campbell, suggested that I take on this project. Lynn Gibson saved me from writer's block. And last on the list, but first everywhere else, come my husband Don and daughter Katriona, whose support never waivers and on whom I rely more than I can say. To all, my thanks.

INTRODUCTION

Writing history is about making decisions. Historians choose from a broad range of subjects, selecting those they think are most important. They choose source materials carefully, assessing evidence that may support or contradict their arguments. And they choose ways to write, balancing respect for their subjects with the needs of their audience.

The best historians make choices so well that they can transform painstaking research into seamless arguments and narratives. But don't be fooled. On the surface history may seem straightforward, but the process of writing is filled with difficult decisions. As Peter Novick says in *That Noble Dream*, writing history, even with the best sources and methods, can be like trying "to nail jelly to a wall."[1] For this reason, historians experiment with many approaches to the past. Still, in the end they must choose an approach that suits their subject.

Ever since the days of the ancient Greeks, the process of selection has guided Western historical writing. Around 404 BCE, when the Athenian general Thucydides composed his history of the Peloponnesian Wars, he could not write about everything that had occurred in the thirty years of battles and defeats. Instead, he wrote an account that emphasized decisive moments, such as Pericles' famous eulogy for the Athenian dead. According to Thucydides, Pericles said:

> I have no wish to make a long speech on subjects familiar to you all: so I shall say nothing about the warlike deeds by which we acquired our power or the battles in which we or our fathers gallantly resisted our enemies, Greek or foreign.

What I want to do is, in the first place, to discuss the spirit in which we faced our trials and also our constitution and the way of life which has made us great. After that I shall speak in praise of the dead. . . .[2]

Thucydides did not just include Pericles' eulogy because it was moving; he recounted the speech because he found it instructive. Like Thucydides, modern-day historians also choose topics that shed light on contemporary problems. In 1987 Paul Kennedy, a history professor at Yale, published a book called *The Rise and Fall of the Great Powers*, in which he argued that great powers rise relative to other powers when they can harness powerful armies and navies to dynamic economies. Kennedy looked to the rise and fall of Habsburg Spain, Bourbon France, and the British Empire to illustrate his point. The implications for world politics were clear, particularly in the 1988 American election year: if America did not preserve its economic power, then it would lose its international dominance.[3]

Like Kennedy and Thucydides, historians choose subjects that they find important, and they explore these important subjects to seek the causes of change over time. To do this, historians choose from many possible methods. Enter the stacks of a library and browse through any shelf of history books. Notice that historians who work in narrow geographical and chronological specialties approach their subjects from a wide variety of perspectives. When historians write, they incorporate methods and insights from the work of other historians as well as from scholarship in the humanities, the natural sciences, and the social sciences. For example, in *"I Have Lived Here Since the World Began"* Arthur Ray used geography, literature, anthropology, and economics to recount the history of Canada's First Nations.[4] Historians choose from so many different approaches that it is difficult to place historical writing in facile categories.

Despite the diversity in historical writing, most historians share a commitment to good writing. Historians learn how to find sources and they know how to report on sources faithfully. Using their sources, they make inferences about the events of the past, then they develop their inferences into sustained arguments and narratives. These must, in turn, be shaped by the conventions for writing good sentences and choosing appropriate words. Historians aspire to communicate their ideas about the past. They try to do so accurately and honestly.

⚔ 1 ⚔

GETTING STARTED

There are many reasons to write history. Historians may be interested in explaining a particular source, in which case they must assess its significance in light of other sources. Perhaps they begin with an analytical problem that they have noticed in some body of historical literature, and they must seek out sources as a way of exploring the problem. Or, more prosaically, an instructor may assign them to write about a particular source or analytical problem; in this case the choices are limited. In any case, the only way to write history is to engage with source materials and other writers. This is challenging because it is not always a simple matter to find suitable sources and to engage the right writers.

Explore Your Interests

People are probably asking you about your interests all the time. At a party, you might find that the best approach is to condense your interests into a crisp one-liner. When you write history, you will grapple with topics and questions that cannot be summarized so neatly. Writing projects present opportunities to clarify and develop your interests.

Historians become interested in research topics for all sorts of reasons. The history of medicine may interest you because you want to become a doctor; the history of physics may interest you because

you are concerned about nuclear proliferation. Perhaps some historians have inspired your interests, either through their teaching or
their writing. Or an instructor may be requiring you to write about
a specific topic (which means that you may not wish to read the following section on how to begin a research project). When you work
on any writing project, use your sources to address questions that are
significant to you.

Move from a Historical Interest
to a Research Topic

There is so much history to write about, and so little time for writing. Deadlines put pressure on everyone, but it is possible to use this
pressure to your advantage. The first thing to do is to convert your
historical interests into a feasible research topic. Find a small story
within your broad range of interests, and select only the best sources,
especially if you have a strict page limit.

There are ways to limit your topic if you find a lot of sources.
Think about what it is, specifically, that you enjoy learning about.
Let us say that during your first year in college your favorite course
was a survey of the history of astronomy. As a child you learned the
names of the stars, and when you were a teenager you were capti-
vated by Carl Sagan's television series, Cosmos. Your course in the
history of astronomy built on this interest, introducing you to the
scientific and practical consequences of astronomical knowledge,
and also to the ways in which this knowledge has changed over
time. Navigation, for example, depends on the accurate measurement of the motion of the earth, sun, and stars, but before the eighteenth century it was very difficult to determine an exact position
on land or at sea. Wouldn't it be great to write an essay on the history of navigation?

Unfortunately, this is the sort of topic that is best suited to a
massive textbook and not to a short essay. Chances are that you
have limits to your time and number of pages. How can you find a
topic that will help you explore your interests but that will also ac-
commodate your limitations? The resources in the library can help
you to narrow down your topic.

Use Print Sources to Begin a Project

Visit the reading room of any good library and you will find fundamental reference works, including encyclopedias, dictionaries, and
textbooks that survey a broad range of interests and topics. Increasingly, encyclopedias and dictionaries are becoming available as
CD-ROMs, and many references are accessible over the Internet.

1. Encyclopedias. A strong encyclopedia can help you to get
an early, broad understanding of a topic. It will contain basic explanations as well as hints about related subjects. Just keep in mind
that encyclopedias can only provide an introduction. If you write a
paper based on encyclopedia articles, you will not impress your
readers.

Nevertheless, the *Encyclopedia Britannica* does contain a useful,
ten-page summary of the history of navigation, stretching from the
earliest development of marine navigation to the recent development of global positioning satellites. The encyclopedia article contains general and technical overviews of the basic problems of navigation and their solutions, as well as illustrations and a bibliography.
In this instance, an encyclopedia article could help to jump-start a
research project.

2. Dictionaries. Dictionaries also provide a quick way to explore some topics. Be aware that there are three different types of
dictionaries, each of which has its own special uses. *Prescriptive* dictionaries like *Webster's* will tell you how words should be used; *descriptive* dictionaries like the *Canadian Oxford Dictionary* will tell
you how words are actually used; *historical* dictionaries like the *Oxford English Dictionary* will tell you how words have been used over
time. Some dictionaries, such as *The Gage Canadian Dictionary*, include both prescriptive and descriptive features.

In the case of navigation, dictionaries probably have little to offer, but they are still worth a look because you never know what you
might find. The meaning of "navigation" is clear enough, and so are
its origins, from the Latin *navis* for ship. As it turns out, the *Oxford
English Dictionary* describes eight different shades of meaning for the
word "navigation," some dating to the sixteenth century. Even so,

in this case the dictionary does not raise any interesting research questions.

3. Textbooks. Textbooks often contain useful surveys of a topic, and they also contain bibliographies. For information on navigation, for example, various types of textbooks might prove to be useful. A world history textbook or a history of science textbook might make reference to changes in navigational methods over time. A textbook on astronomy or navigation might provide you with helpful technical explanations. Check textbook bibliographies for further references.

Sources for Canadian History

A wide variety of reference works and bibliographies on Canadian topics are available in most college and university libraries, and these can be useful first steps in your topic search and your further research. General bibliographies include *Canadian History: A Reader's Guide*, *The Oxford Companion to Canadian History and Literature* (and its *Supplement*), *Bibliographia Canadiana*, and *Writing About Canada: A Handbook for Modern Canadian History*.[5] In addition to the simple listing of bibliographical sources under topic areas, many of these works contain articles on places, individuals, groups, political parties, governmental policies, business affairs and so on. You might also check to see whether your library has any more general historical bibliographies, such as the *Annual Bulletin of the Historical Association*, a British publication that includes analyses of recent books, journals and journal articles, including sections on specific time periods and one on "the Americas."[6]

Once you have an idea of a more specific area for your research, you might also check for specialized bibliographies. If you were interested in women's history, for example, you could look at *Changing Women, Changing History: A Bibliography of the History of Women in Canada*. If First Nations' history were your interest, you would want to check references such as *The Ethnographic Bibliography of North America*. Perhaps you are interested in regional history? In this case you might find books such as *A Bibliography of British Columbia* or, for an even more local example, *The Vancouver Centennial Bibliography*.[7]

Canadian scholars can also take advantage of a host of reference works, and these can be particularly useful once one has a topic area to follow. In this category we would list, for example, *The Canadian Encyclopedia* (also available on-line), *The Dictionary of Canadian Biography* and *The Collins Dictionary of Canadian History*.[8] In many cases the articles in these books also contain lists of additional sources, so be sure to check these also for further ideas. Another important reference to consult is the *Historical Atlas of Canada*, which has been published in a three-volume set as well as a concise edition, and which includes short articles and bibliographies for most of its maps.[9] You might also find regional or local encyclopedias and atlases that are relevant for your topic.

Periodicals and scholarly journals can also be valuable sources for Canadian history. Probably the best way to search for articles on your topic is to search the various periodical indexes. These list articles from journals, magazines and newspapers, and they are arranged alphabetically by subject as well as by author. Most college libraries carry *The Canadian Periodical Index*, *The Canadian Magazine Index*, and *The Canadian Index*, all of which are reasonably easy to use. If you find articles in journals that your institution does not carry, inter-library loans are usually possible. Some Canadian historical journals, such as *The Canadian Historical Review*, also have their own indexes for ease of research. Also remember to check whether there are any specialized journals appropriate for your topic. Journals such as *Urban History Review*, *Prairie Forum*, *Newfoundland Studies*, and *Labour/LeTravail* fall into this category.

Finally, a word about electronic searches and sources. A wide variety of online sites either deal with Canadian history sources explicitly or can lead you to them less directly. In the former category, for instance, the National Library of Canada runs a bibliographical site that lists specifically Canadian and American topics and titles. You can find this site at www.n/c-bnc.ca/amicus/. Less specific to Canada, but extremely useful, are search engines such as EBSCO Host and other search sites that give you access to articles, some in full text, from a huge variety of journals. The ELN Serials Union Database can tell you where to find journals to which your library does not subscribe. If you are unsure how to conduct electronic searches, remember that reference librarians are real experts on this, and they will generally be pleased to show you how to launch your online search. For more on librarians and electronic searches, see the sections later in this chapter.

The *A.H.A.* Guide

A good way to learn about reference sources is to look in *The American Historical Association's Guide to Historical Literature*, edited by Mary Beth Norton and Pamela Gerardi.[10] It is the most useful reference guide for almost every historian beginning a new project, and it is owned by many college libraries. The *A.H.A. Guide*, as it is called, is organized into commonly recognized historical fields of specialization, such as "Central Asia," "Canada," and "International Relations since 1920." Open to the table of contents to find your own area of interest, then turn to the part of the guide that contains your broad area of interest. First you will find a short essay by a specialist, describing the main research problems in the field. Next you will find a table of contents for the field, and you will also see that the field is broken down into subcategories. Under each subcategory the editors have listed the most significant works of scholarship in the field. They provide bibliographic details, but they also summarize each work briefly.

Naturally, these are subjective selections on the part of the editors, but the works listed in the bibliography can give a beginning researcher a strong head start. And each section of the *A.H.A. Guide* begins with a list of other reference works that might help you if you cannot find clues within the *Guide*. Almost every broad subject in history has its own special reference works, and these might help you to find more sources.

Conduct a search for "Navigation" in the *A.H.A. Guide*. The main table of contents indicates that there is a section on "Science, Technology, and Medicine" on page 77. Turn there, and the first thing you will find is an essay by Robert Dekosky that provides a broad survey of the main issues in the history of science, technology, and medicine. Then, on page 81, Dekosky provides a table of contents for the section, listing subheadings. Some are definitely worth checking. Your first stop should be the subheading on reference works, and next take a look at several other subheadings that might be related to navigation: "Modern Astronomy, Cosmology, and Astrophysics," "Scientific Instruments," and "Naval and Maritime Technology."

Turn next to each of these subheadings. The descriptions of other reference guides seem especially promising. You learn that historians of science and technology are fortunate that the editors of the scholarly journals *Isis* and *Technology and Culture* compile annual bibliographies on all subjects relating to the history of science and technology. The bibliographies before 1976 are available in hard copy, and the bibliographies after 1976 are available in both hard copy and CD-ROM. This is just one example of the treasure trove of information available in the *A.H.A. Guide*. If you were conducting research on another topic, you would find that other specific bibliographies are listed, such as *Historical Abstracts* and *America: History and Life*. No matter what you are researching, use the *A.H.A. Guide* to identify the principal bibliographies and works in the field.

Look carefully through the *A.H.A. Guide*. After scanning the reference subheading, you find that the "Modern Astronomy, Cosmology, and Astrophysics" section does not seem to contain any references that can help you, and neither does the subheading on "Naval and Maritime Technology." But the subheading on "Scientific Instruments" does list a number of interesting titles. Based on what you have found in the *A.H.A. Guide*, it is now time to search for the most promising works, and also to search the bibliographies from *Isis* and *Technology and Culture*.

Speak with a Librarian

Librarians are the unsung heroes of the historical world. Historians depend on librarians heavily, and together with librarians historians share a commitment to preserving information. Librarians know how to organize that information, and can therefore help historians find things. When in doubt, ask a librarian.

In the case of navigation, almost any librarian would have known, without looking in the *A.H.A. Guide*, that the main bibliographies in the history of science and technology are compiled by *Isis* and *Technology and Culture*. Librarians would probably not be familiar with the other sources listed in the *A.H.A. Guide*, but they would have known to tell you to look in the *A.H.A. Guide*. Librarians also know other ways to search for bibliographies and basic reference works, even in the absence of an *A.H.A. Guide*.

Use Electronic Resources in the Library

When performing historical research, the time will come when you find that you have exhausted the reference collection of your library's reading room. You will have accumulated a list of titles, but you will need to start looking in the library catalogue for the titles of books that are kept in the stacks. If you still do not feel comfortable searching your library's catalogue, ask a librarian for help.

Start to Explore Your Library's Catalogue. Library catalogues can be a tremendous help in your search for works on a subject. Most catalogues are now computerized and accessible online. The key to searching a computerized catalogue is understanding the way in which the information is organized. Most items in the library have an author, a title, or a subject heading. In order to find the right headings, start with a keyword search. In a keyword search, it is important to use distinctive words. Type in "longitude," and you will get many entries. A narrower set of entries will be revealed if your keyword search includes the following unique words: "longitude history harrison." This keyword search will bring you to several works, each of which will have subject headings. Click on the subject headings to link to other works on the same subject. Please note that subject searches are different from keyword searches. Keyword searches may turn up your word or words in many different orders. By contrast, subject headings are fixed by the Library of Congress. You will only "hit" a subject heading if you type in its exact wording. (All librarians will be able to explain to you how to search for Library of Congress subject headings.) Once you come across a useful subject heading, follow links to other subjects. Click on author and title links to help identify related works.

Explore Other Library Resources That Are Online. Libraries subscribe to many different online services. Small college libraries cannot afford the kinds of subscriptions that are available to historians at big research universities. Even so, there are several types of services that are commonly available. Encyclopedias and dictionaries are now often available online. So are back issues of historical journals, thanks to Project Muse and JSTOR. Indexes of articles and unpublished dissertations are also available by library subscription. Be aware that computerized indexes may not list articles that were written before the 1980s. Also be aware that these indexes may be one or two years out of date. In most instances, it pays to check the "hard copy" indexes and tables of contents for very old and very new titles. Some online index search services, like

ProQuest, FirstSearch, and EBSCO, will search through multiple databases that used to exist only in print form, such as Books In Print, Dissertation Abstracts, Humanities Index, and Social Science Index. Some online search services even deliver the full texts of articles. If articles are not immediately available, they may be requested through Interlibrary Loan. Some Interlibrary Loan services now deliver articles electronically.

Be Skeptical About Other Online Resources

One of the good things about beginning an electronic search with library resources is that librarians will only make available catalogues, indexes, and references that are worthwhile. Though there are many worthy sources available online that lie beyond the library's website, out on the World Wide Web, there are also many unworthy sites. The trick is to distinguish between the worthy and the unworthy.

It takes a great deal of time and effort to publish a book or journal article. Typically, works of history that are published must meet with the approval of editors and peer reviewers before they are printed and distributed. For this reason, many students have gotten into the habit of trusting published sources. However, publishing on the Internet can be done cheaply and quickly, with no controls for quality. There are virtually no barriers to publishing a website.

The best way to look for a website is to use a high-quality search engine. Today many academics prefer the Google search engine, at <http://www.google.com>. Other search engines exist, too, and many more may be added in the next few years. Many of the same principles used to search electronic library catalogues apply to search engines, too. (Check the search engine's home page for advice on how it looks for websites.) Search for keywords by using distinctive words. Then, when you have some results, don't just click on the first two or three Internet addresses; scrutinize the entire list of "hits." Search engines do not necessarily organize their results in terms of quality.

There are a number of ways to determine the quality of a website.

Remember the basics.   While you are looking at the site, note the address, the author, the title, the owner of the domain, and the date of publication. Not only will this help you to evaluate the site, it will also help you to give a proper citation later, when you are writing.

Beware of domain names. Websites that contain <.edu>, <.ac>, <.gov>, or <.org> were created by people affiliated with academic, government, or non-profit institutions. At the very least, the authors of the sites had to be accepted or hired by the institutions. At most, these websites may represent the views of these organizations. On the subject of longitude, there is one such institutional website: England's Royal Observatory, located at the National Maritime Museum, Greenwich, has published a highly informative website, complete with illustrations: <http://www.rog.nmm.ac.uk/museum/harrison/index.html>. By contrast to this site, which contains <.ac>, websites containing <.com> or <.co> are commercial sites. Anybody with a credit card can publish one. This is not to say that all commercial sites are bad, or all academic sites are good, but this is one way to begin to verify the information on a website. The suffixes <.ca> (Canada) and <.uk> (United Kingdom) are used by commercial, governmental, and academic sites.

Ask if the website has also been published in print. There are many sites that began as print sources, or are published in both print and electronic editions. In these cases, the quality is likely to be higher, because print tends to have higher quality controls.

Ask if the information on the website is available elsewhere. There are now some outstanding websites published by historical archives. In these cases, it would be possible to travel to the archives to verify the information published online. In the case of eighteenth-century British navigation, one such source would be the journal of Sir Joseph Banks, who traveled with Captain Cook and kept a record of their discoveries in Australia. Banks's journals can be found online at <http://www.sl.nsw.gov.au/banks/> thanks to the State Library of New South Wales, Australia.

Assess the website skeptically. There are wonderful websites that are very useful for historians. There are also websites that are utterly useless, and many that are just mediocre. How can you tell the difference? Assess the tone of the website. Is it scholarly, or is it ranting? Does it present evidence that can be verified, or does it make claims that are unverifiable? Is it written by scholars whose names and affiliations you recognize, or is it written by people without reputations?

When in doubt, speak with your professor. None of the criteria listed above can be used as the sole determinant of a website's reliability. Taken together, they can help. If you still have doubts about historical sources that you have found on the Internet, present your source to your professor, even just by sending an e-mail message containing the Internet address of the website in question. It is better to ask about a source before you write the paper, than to be asked about it after you have turned the paper in.

Approach Your Topic from a Particular Angle

A library at a large university will probably contain more than a thousand items on navigation, and it may also have special collections of manuscripts and artifacts. Even a small library may have several dozen items on navigation. Don't be discouraged. You simply need to bring more focus to your topic.

Think back to the books you have read and the courses you have taken. If you like to read biographies, then you might want to identify an individual who made a significant contribution to the field. If you like to read social history, you might wish to explore a topic along the lines of class, gender, or race. You might be partial to the history of a particular place or time period. Keep working in the library reference room until it seems that you have a manageable number of resources with which to write an essay on a reasonably focused topic.

Imagine that you are still interested in writing about the history of navigation. In the past you enjoyed reading about the adventures of eighteenth-century British sea captains like Bligh, Cook, and Vancouver. While searching your library catalogue, you decide to find a biography of one of these captains, to see if it tells anything about navigation. You search the catalogue for Captain James Cook, which reveals many items. You skim the list, looking for a substantial, recent biography, and you find J.C. Beaglehole's *The Life of Captain James Cook*, published in 1974. This book might contain important clues.

Go to the Library and Do Some Background Reading

Searching cannot be done exclusively from a computer terminal or a card catalogue. It is time to go to the stacks of the library. Locate Beaglehole's book on Captain Cook and skim the index to see if it mentions the science of navigation. You will find that on pages 109 to 117, Beaglehole discusses how eighteenth-century sea captains had a very difficult time calculating their longitude. Here is a specific problem in the history of navigation: how to use celestial observations and mathematical calculations to determine a position and plot a course. Now you might have a specific topic. You also have an additional word for searching, "longitude."

As you define your topic, you will find yourself moving back and forth between searching in the catalogue and reading in the stacks. Go back to the catalogue and search under "Longitude." Here you also find many items, but as you work your way through the entries, you notice, under the subject "Longitude," a promising subheading: "Longitude—Measurement—History." Here there are only a few items, one of which meets your needs particularly well. It is Dava Sobel's small book, *Longitude: The True Story of a Lone Genius Who Solved the Greatest Scientific Problem of His Time* (New York: Walker, 1995). When you find it in the library stacks, you see that it is a concise book that summarizes the scientific problems surrounding longitude. It also tells the story of John Harrison, the clockmaker who struggled against great odds to build the first marine chronometer, the essential instrument for calculating longitude. Sobel's book is a popular account that lacks footnotes, but it does contain a useful short bibliography.

Under the same subject heading, you also find a book called *The Quest for Longitude*, edited by William Andrewes, which summarizes the proceedings of a historical conference held at Harvard in 1993. The book contains numerous illustrations and technical discussions, but most important for your present purposes, it also contains a number of scholarly articles on longitude, as well as substantial footnotes and an extensive bibliography. Now you have two recent sources that can point you in further directions.

Browse for More Sources

There is only one way to make an informed choice about a topic: go to the library stacks and browse through the potential source materials. Look for both quantity and quality. Are there enough sources to write this paper, or are there so many sources that the topic must be narrowed further? It is also important to consider when your sources were published. Are you finding the most recent scholarship, or do your sources seem old enough to be out of date? Are your sources so old that they are from the period of time that you are studying?

In the case of longitude, the Sobel and Andrewes bibliographies are sufficient to be used as guides to identifying sources. Both books were published recently, and both contain fairly comprehensive bibliographies. It is probably a good idea to start with a narrow base of sources and build it into a broader base. Therefore, try to find some of the sources in Sobel's short bibliography, and as you dig more deeply, draw on Andrewes's longer bibliography. As you search for sources in the library stacks, you will find more clues that will lead you to further sources. Just keep in mind that there are limits to your time and there are limits to your paper. In the early stages of research you do not need to find everything.

Form a Hypothesis

An essay based on historical research should reach new conclusions about a topic. This is a challenging proposition, and by now you may be wondering if it is worth writing a paper about longitude at all. Sobel and her predecessors have already written plenty about the subject. Can you bring a unique perspective to bear on longitude?

While you are identifying a topic, you should begin forming a hypothesis, one of the most important steps in writing a research paper. A hypothesis is not an ordinary question; it is the question that can guide you through the research. As you read through your sources you will ask for answers to your hypothesis, and as you get answers you will refine your hypothesis. As you do this over the course of your research, you will find that you are getting closer to forming an argument.

How does one arrive at a hypothesis? Start to jot down some questions. In the case of longitude, you may be wondering about the following things: (1) What sort of person was Harrison? (2) What distinguished Harrison's clocks from other clocks? (3) How serious was the problem of finding longitude? (4) Was Harrison really a lone genius, as Sobel says, or did he have collaborators?

Now ask yourself two more things: Can you build an argument around the potential answer to one of the questions, and does the question address some broader issue in history? Questions 1 and 2 might yield only descriptions and not arguments. Question 3 could produce a debate (Yes, longitude was a serious problem; No, it wasn't so serious), but such a debate, although it might have been important during the eighteenth century, would not occur today among historians. Question 4 seems a bit more promising. Answers to it could either support or reject Sobel's interpretation. They might also help you to ask questions about the social dimensions of scientific research, a common approach for a historian.

Craft a Proposal

After you have completed your preliminary research, craft a one-page proposal. Your teachers and friends will probably be happy to read it and comment on it. Even if they are not, the process of writing the proposal will still help you to sketch out your ideas. The proposal is an early opportunity to think critically about your topic.

Every proposal should answer these questions:

1. What is your topic? Describe it briefly.
2. What is your hypothesis? Tell which question is driving your research.
3. What will your readers learn from this project? Will you be bringing new information to light, or will you be interpreting commonplace knowledge in a new way?
4. Why is your project significant or interesting? Discuss the relationship between your project and some broader issue in history.
5. What are your principal sources? Give a short bibliography.
6. What methods will you use to evaluate your sources? Will you be reading library books or will you be using archival materials? Will you be analyzing objects and paintings? Are any of

your sources in foreign languages, and if so, can you understand them? Will you be using methods from another discipline, such as sociology?

Write an Annotated Bibliography

Your object at the next stage of your project should be to compile an annotated bibliography. This exercise will help you assess the breadth and significance of your sources. Arrange your sources according to the instructions for a bibliography given at the end of Chapter 3 of this volume. After each entry in your bibliography, summarize the source and state why you will be using it in your paper. Describe any special circumstances surrounding the source. You should keep your notes on sources concise, but you may wish to say more about some sources than others.

An annotated bibliography on longitude might contain the following entries:

Quill, Humphrey. *John Harrison, the Man Who Found Longitude.* London: Baker, 1966. Quill has written a biography of John Harrison, the eighteenth-century English clockmaker. Harrison built the first marine chronometer, thus solving the problem of how to calculate longitude. Quill respects Harrison's achievements but also criticizes the clockmaker's irascible behavior, particularly during his interactions with professional astronomers.

Sobel, Dava. *Longitude: The True Story of a Lone Genius Who Solved the Greatest Scientific Problem of His Time.* New York: Walker & Co., 1995. Sobel has written a biography of Harrison that is dramatic and filled with adulation. Sobel argues that Harrison was a hero who triumphed in the face of unreasonable opposition from professional astronomers.

Talk to People About Your Topic

Don't be bashful. Talk with other people about your topic, including your teachers and friends. It can also be interesting to seek out experts in your area of interest. Experts are usually happy to discuss specific research problems with other researchers, especially when they are presented with thoughtful questions and written proposals. If the experts happen to be history professors, visit them during their office hours, or make appointments to see them. You may also wish to seek out experts in other departments of a university, and outside of universities too. For example, if you were to conduct research on longitude, you might wish to write to some of the authors working in the field. You might also try to find some navigational equipment, and ask someone to show you how to use it.

If You Have to Abandon a Topic, Do It Early

The process of finding sources, forming a hypothesis, and crafting a proposal will test the viability of your topic. If at the end of a week or two you no longer want to work on your topic, then find another one. There are plenty of reasons to stop working on a topic. You may not find enough sources, or you may decide that the topic is less interesting than you had thought. It is better to bail out of a bad project early than to go down in flames later.

INTERPRETING SOURCE MATERIALS

When you write history, you will know that the sources all relate to a particular topic, but you will have to decide how to interpret and assemble them. At first you might find the sources confusing and even contradictory. Historical writing resembles detective work because sources often raise more questions than they answer. Sometimes they lead historians on exhilarating wild-goose chases that culminate in dead ends. Other times they enable historians to slowly recover unexpected tales from the past. Fortunately there are many ways to assess source materials.

Work Systematically

Historians do not make random choices. Historians work as systematically as possible, and they even share rules for selecting evidence with writers across the disciplines. Some of these rules even date back to the ancient Greeks. Hippocrates' advice to Greek doctors might well apply to today's historians:

> In Medicine one must pay attention not to plausible theorizing but to experience and reason together . . . I agree that

19

theorizing is to be approved, provided that it is based on facts, and systematically makes its deductions from what is observed . . . But conclusions drawn by the unaided reason can hardly be serviceable; only those drawn from observed facts.[11]

Ever since the days of the ancient Greeks, historians and other writers have debated some of these fundamental notions: What is plausible theorizing? Is the difference between reason and irrationality simply a matter of objective systematization, or does reason have to be subjectively "approved," "observed," and "aided" by people? Historians have often written about these questions, not only to understand ancient Greek scientists but also to understand how to write history.

Distinguish Primary Sources from Secondary Works

Sources drive all histories, but all sources are not created equal. As a matter of convenience, historians distinguish between primary sources and secondary works.

   1. *Primary Sources.* Primary sources originate in the time period that historians are studying. They vary a great deal. They may include personal memoirs, government documents, transcripts of legal proceedings, oral histories and traditions, archaeological and biological evidence, and visual sources like paintings and photographs. It is likely that these types of primary sources will be very important to your project.

   Each kind of primary source must be considered on its own terms. Historians used to think that some source materials were inherently more reliable than others. Leopold von Ranke, the founder of modern, professional history, considered government documents to be the gold standard of all primary sources. But even government documents are subjective in some way. Like all sources, they reveal some things but remain silent on others.

   2. *Secondary Works.* Secondary works reflect on earlier times. Typically, they are books and articles by writers who are interpreting the events and primary sources that you are studying. Secondary works vary a great deal, from books by professional scholars to journalistic accounts. Evaluate each secondary work on its own merits, particularly on how well it uses primary sources as evidence. In some cases this distinction between primary sources and secondary works may be confusing. If you are writing about historical writers, you may find yourself using a secondary work as a primary source. For example, during the 1840s and 1850s Thomas Babington Macaulay wrote *The History of England*. His book describes the origins and outcome of England's Glorious Revolution of 1688. For historians of seventeenth-century England, Macaulay's book is a classic secondary work. But for historians of Victorian Britain, *The History of England* is a rich primary source that tells historians a great deal about intellectual life in the 1840s and 1850s.

Refine Your Hypothesis with Who, What, Why, Where, and When

While you are reading each source, you should be asking how the source might support or contradict your hypothesis. Pretty soon, you will have a lot of information that relates to your hypothesis. Organize your answers around the journalist's questions: who, what, why, where, when.

Newspaper reporters tell beginning reporters to ask these questions when they are reporting a story. Historian Richard Marius began his career as a journalist, and in his *Short Guide to Writing about History* he advises students to ask these reporter's questions when they read source materials. It is good advice. Answers to these questions can be very complex, depending on the sources and the story.[12] Take notes and use your answers to help you form ideas for your essay.

Imagine for a moment that you are writing a biography of Louis Riel, and that your sources consist mainly of nineteenth-century archival materials. To get through these sources, you have formed a hypothesis: Riel's militancy did not represent the majority political view on the South Saskatchewan River in 1884–5. As you read about all of Riel's decisions, consider organizing your research around the reporter's questions. When you start to get answers, take notes.

The "Who" Question.   Historians ask "who" to learn biographical information about significant actors, to learn who bore the brunt of historical changes, and to learn who caused things to happen. In your biography of Riel, you could use the sources to make yourself familiar with all the main characters. What groups made up the South Saskatchewan community? Who actively supported Riel? Who actively opposed him? Who remained on the fringes of activism?

The "What" Question.   Different sources often describe the same events differently. Know each version of events so that you can compare accounts. Let us say that you are focusing momentarily on Riel's decision to return to the North-West in 1884. What did he understand of the situation and population there? How well did he understand the wider political realities after living in the US for some years? What did he do to gain knowledge of the situation? What did he do to gain support for his decisions and actions? What were the strategic and political consequences of his return?

The "Why" Question.   Why did some things change while others remained the same? Using each source, make a list of possible causes. Try to distinguish the most significant causes of events from the background causes. Why was Riel successful in his 1870 rebellion, but not in 1885? Did the answer lie in himself, in others, or in the changed circumstances? Was his leadership less effective in 1885? Had he himself changed? Was the level or the quality of his support different? Was the response from the federal government different?

The "Where" Question.   Sometimes you will find fairly self-evident answers to the "where" question. Other times geographical considerations will open your eyes to unexpected circumstances. You might even find it helpful to draw a map of your subject. Where, for example, is Batoche? Was this a wise choice for his headquarters? Might a stronger stand have been made elsewhere? What was the route of the new railway? Did this specific route make a difference to the outcome of events?

The "When" Question. Historians analyze change and continuity over time. Not surprisingly, it becomes quite important to know when historical events happened. Depending on the topic, you may get an easy answer or no answer at all. Try as much as you can to determine when things happened. Use this information to place events in a chronological relationship. Try to make one timeline from all your source materials so that you may understand the order of events. When, for example, did Riel decide to move from petitions and diplomatic appeals to armed resistance? If he had made this decision earlier, might the outcome have been different, or would the federal government have been able to respond with troops just as quickly anyway?

Be Sensitive to Points of View in Your Sources

As you use your hypothesis to work your way through the source materials, you will come to see that many sources present history from a certain point of view. Even photographs show only the perspective of the photographer. Photographers have even been known to arrange their pictures, and their mere presence with a camera changes how their subjects behave. How then do historians know which sources to trust?

Historians must be sensitive to the ways in which sources come to be available. Why is only some information available? Chroniclers record events as they happen but they describe only the things they consider to be important. For example, in a book called *Silencing the Past*, Rolph Trouillot mentions that Caribbean slave-owners usually kept detailed records of their plantations, but sometimes the slave-owners neglected to record births. Infant mortality was so high on some plantations that it was not worth the trouble to add a new slave child to the registers until the baby survived to a certain age. Therefore, these records lack important data. Historians may wish to reconstruct the history of Caribbean slave families, but the plantation chronicles make it a difficult task. Chroniclers use their own contemporary standards when they decide to record certain events and to keep silent about others.[13]

The process of producing sources does not end with the selections of the chroniclers. All sorts of factors determine whether or not chronicles will survive. Sometimes wars, fires, and floods can silence

the past. But most of the time, collectors, archivists, and librarians
decide to preserve some chronicles and to discard others. They have
their own visions of the past, and politics and economics can influence their decisions in many ways. For example, during the 1960s
Loren Graham began to collect information about a Soviet engineer
named Peter Palchinsky, who was executed by Stalin in 1929. Graham believed that Palchinsky had made significant contributions to
early Soviet engineering, but the Soviet government was hiding
Palchinsky's papers from researchers because the engineer had criti-
cized the regime. Graham had to wait almost thirty years, but when
the Soviet Union collapsed he finally gained access to Palchinsky's
papers. Then, in a nice twist of fate, Graham found that the Palchinsky papers could help him to write a book that explained, in part, the
Soviet Union's failure. His quest for sources became a subplot of his
history, *The Ghost of the Executed Engineer*.[14] But even in Graham's
case, the selections of chroniclers influenced the writing of history.

Select the Most Important Source Materials

You cannot include everything in your essay. You must select the
information that you need to make your point, even if that means
neglecting potentially interesting tangents. Historians are not just
collectors of facts, they are selectors and arrangers. They function
like the human memory, remembering some things and forgetting
others. Try not to be like the main character in Jorge Luis Borges's
story "Funes, the Memorious":

> He remembered the shapes of the clouds in the south at dawn
> on the 30th of April of 1882, and he could compare them in
> his recollection with the marbled grain in the design of a
> leather-bound book which he had seen only once, and with
> the lines in the spray which an oar raised in the Rio Negro on
> the eve of the battle of Quebracho . . . He told me . . . My
> memory, sir, is like a garbage disposal.[15]

Historians exercise selectivity with sources so that they may avoid
producing garbage disposals. Some information will be significant to
an essay, but much will be insignificant. Don't feel bad if you spend
a lot of time interpreting a source, only to find that it does not con-

tribute to your essay's main idea. It is tempting to include such sources, if only to show your readers how hard you have been working, but some sources are bound to be irrelevant. In the end, a coherent essay will impress readers more than a garbage disposal.

Take Notes by Being Selective

When you first begin to analyze your sources, you will need to take notes. When historians take notes, they take advantage of a number of techniques: some historians use index cards and notebook paper, while others use word-processing programs or even database programs. Choosing a method of taking notes depends to a great extent on the type of research you are conducting, and it is often a matter of personal preference. As you conduct more research, you will get a better sense of how you prefer to take notes.

All note-taking methods, whether low-tech or high-tech, present a common difficulty: how to select the most important material for your notes. Usually, you do not want to copy your sources word for word. You want to write down only the information that is likely to be useful in your essay. But how do you know what is going to be useful before you even write the essay? Reaching this decision is the most difficult part of note-taking. You want to write down useful information, but you recognize that some information that appears to be useless now may turn out to be useful later.

It is difficult to know in advance which notes will be useful. It is for this reason that you should use your hypothesis to help you read sources. Ask yourself how a source relates to your hypothesis, and jot down notes from the source that answer fundamental questions about your hypothesis. Use your hypothesis to help select the most important information from your sources.

The trickiest thing about using a hypothesis during note-taking is that your hypothesis is likely to change. This is as it should be. Over the course of your research you will refine your ideas about your sources, and your hypothesis will get closer and closer to a thesis or argument. Unfortunately, this also means that your early notes will be more extensive and less useful than your later notes. Don't be disappointed if, at the end of a project, you find that you have taken some extraneous notes: it is a natural consequence of refining a hypothesis and being selective.

⇥ *3* ⇤

WRITING HISTORY FAITHFULLY

In the first century BCE, Cicero said, "The first law for the historian is that he shall never dare utter an untruth. The second is that he shall suppress nothing that is true."[16] The spirit of these laws remains the same, even if some of the conventions for writing history have changed.

Good historical writers always question authorities, even formidable ones like Cicero. One question comes immediately to mind: how do historians know what is true? Historians may never know the answer to such a question because sources often present contradictions and silences. Even so, historians recognize certain rules of representing the past faithfully. Like the law, these rules are written down but they are also subject to variation and interpretation over time. Historians do not take a Hippocratic oath to uphold any particular body of rules, but a broad consensus exists among historical writers about what is right and what is wrong.

Collect and Report Your Sources Carefully

There is more to honesty than simply having good intentions. Historians must be faithful to sources by collecting and reporting them carefully. Scholarship relies heavily on trust because scholars all build on the work of others. Above all, it is important to report accurately on the people and events of the past.

Sloppy note-taking can cause you to misrepresent history. Even if your misrepresentations are inadvertent, readers may still accuse you of dishonesty. To avoid any such misunderstanding, apply some basic rules to your note-taking:

1. Every Note Should Contain a Citation. Every time you jot down a note, write the bibliographic reference next to it. Each note card, each computer entry, and each piece of paper should indicate where you got the information. Always include page numbers. If you are pressed for time, do not cut corners in your notes: work out a system of abbreviations.

2. Make a Clear Distinction Between Your Words and Your Source's Words. Always put direct quotations in quotation marks. When you paraphrase someone else's words, make sure that your own words are distinct.

3. Watch Your Word Processor. Ages ago, when historians wrote with rock chisels, quill pens, and manual typewriters, writing and revising drafts was a painful process. Nowadays, word processing makes it easier to compose and revise while you consult sources. This is convenient, but word processors do present some organizational challenges. Always keep your notes in a separate file from your writing. Be especially careful when cutting and pasting source materials from the Internet. If you keep notes and text in the same file, you will run the risk of confusing your own words with someone else's. Writing technology has changed, but the standards for evaluating plagiarism have remained the same.[17]

Incorporate the Ideas of Others with Care and Respect

When you conduct research and write papers, you will have to engage the ideas of fellow scholars. Much of the time you will be interpreting subjects that others have interpreted before you. Even if you are the first person to write a history of something, chances are you will have to place your own ideas in the context of a broader historical literature.

All historians know that writing is hard work. Therefore it is important to acknowledge the work of others in a respectful way. Historians have conventions for quoting, summarizing, and paraphrasing the works of other scholars. Keep these conventions in mind while you are taking notes. That way you will not have to go back and check your sources while you are writing.

Summarize and Paraphrase Fairly

Technically speaking, a paraphrase restates another writer's words in about the same number of words; a summary reduces another writer's words to a more concise number of words. Historical writers often paraphrase and summarize the ideas of others. Paraphrase when you think that it is important to discuss someone else's work but you think you can say the same thing more clearly in about the same number of words. Summarize when you think you can say it more clearly and more concisely, or when the longer version is inappropriate. A summary or a paraphrase indicates to your reader that you have digested another author's work to the point at which you are able to restate it in your own words.

In historical writing, paraphrases are not as common as summaries, but paraphrases still have their uses. They are particularly helpful when you must translate an archaic or complex quotation into standard English. For example, in *To Keep and Bear Arms: The Origins of an Anglo-American Right*, historian Joyce Malcolm analyzes passages from William Blackstone's *Commentaries on the Laws of England*, the eighteenth century's most famous interpretation of the law. Blackstone wrote, "In a land of liberty, it is extremely dangerous to make a distinct order of the profession of arms." Malcolm precedes this slightly archaic quotation with her own paraphrase: "As for standing armies, Blackstone recommended they be treated with utmost caution."[18] Malcolm's paraphrase helps readers to understand Blackstone's somewhat old-fashioned terminology.

A summary of someone else's work is usually more convenient than a paraphrase because historians write to express their own original ideas, even when they are engaging the ideas of others. Summaries are everywhere in historical writing, and they are most common in works of synthesis. In a recent survey of colonial American

social history, *Pursuits of Happiness*, Jack Greene summarizes the
work of Perry Miller, an earlier historian who wrote some classic
studies of New England:

> Although, as Perry Miller has emphasized, New England reli-
> gious culture remained vital and adaptable throughout the
> years from 1670 to 1730, it lost its former preeminence in
> community life.

Greene then summarizes some of Miller's evidence in a few more
brisk sentences. Even though Miller's work was both stimulating and
extensive, Greene has a limited amount of space to devote to it. Still,
he has given a fair summary. Readers who want to know more about
Miller may use Greene's citations as a guide to further reading.[19]

Quote Occasionally

Most often, historians demonstrate their familiarity with sources by
summarizing and paraphrasing, but occasionally they find that a direct quotation is the best way to make a point. Use a direct quotation when the language of your source is vivid and you cannot possibly do justice to it by summarizing or paraphrasing it. Also quote
a source directly when key points of interpretation depend on the
exact wording in the source. Otherwise, try to limit your use of quotations. Readers are reading your writing principally to find out your
own original ideas.

There are two different kinds of quotations. Most of the time
when historians quote, they run the quotation into their own text.
Typically, they begin the sentence by telling the reader who is
speaking; then they insert the quotation. Imagine that you are writing about the nineteenth-century French philosopher Pierre Joseph
Proudhon. You write,

> At a time when the French bourgeoisie was growing, Proud-
> hon was quite brave to declare that "property is theft."

Notice that in this sentence it was not necessary to separate the
body of the sentence from the quotation by using a comma or a
colon. These punctuation marks should be used with a quotation

only when the punctuation is necessary for the grammar and syntax of the sentence.

The second kind of quotation is called a block quotation. When historians need to quote a passage that is longer than three lines, they indent ten spaces from the left margin and type the quotation in a block set off from the text. The sentence before the quotation should introduce it, and the sentence after the quotation should link it to the text that follows. For example, in his pioneering social history, *The Making of the English Working Class*, E.P. Thompson used block quotations to give readers a flavor of English discourse on the subject of labour during the late eighteenth century and early nineteenth century. Thompson used the words of the activist Francis Place to define some key terms. Thompson wrote:

> Such diversity of experiences has led some writers to question both the notions of an "industrial revolution" and of a "working class." The first discussion need not detain us here. The term is serviceable enough in its usual connotations. For the second, many writers prefer the term working *classes*, which emphasises the great disparity in status, acquisitions, skills, conditions within the portmanteau phrase. And in this they echo the complaints of Francis Place:
>> If the character and the conduct of the working people are to be taken from reviews, magazines, pamphlets, newspapers, reports of the two Houses of Parliament and the Factory Commissioners, we shall find them all jumbled together as the "lower orders," the most skilled and the most prudent workman, with the most ignorant and imprudent laborers and paupers, though the difference is great indeed, and indeed in many cases will scarce admit of comparison.
> Place is, of course, right: the Sunderland tailor, the Irish navvy, the Jewish costermonger, the inmate of an East Anglian village workhouse, the compository on *The Times*—all might be seen by their "betters" as belonging to the "lower classes" while they themselves might scarcely understand each other's dialect.[20]

Thompson connects his own ideas to the ideas of Place by seamlessly integrating the block quotation with the preceding and following paragraphs.

Use Ellipses and Brackets, but
Do Justice to Your Sources

When historians insert quotations in their writing, they often abridge the quotation so that it reflects the needs of their own writing more precisely. Historians indicate these changes by marks of ellipsis, which look like three periods (. . .) and also by using square brackets like these: [ ]. One basic rule governs the use of ellipsis and brackets: any abridged quotation must be faithful to the original, full quotation.

This is not as easy as it sounds. Marks of ellipsis and brackets can be tricky to use faithfully. Imagine that you are writing a five-page essay about the 1837 rebellion in Upper Canada. You have decided to analyze the complaints of William Lyon Mackenzie and the other reformers about how King William IV treated the colony. In a newspaper article most likely written by Mackenzie they enumerated a long list of grievances including the following few:

- The King of England has forbidden his governors to pass laws of immediate and pressing importance, unless suspended in their operation till his assent should be obtained; and when so suspended, he has utterly neglected to attend to them. He has interfered with the freedom of elections, and appointed elections to be held at places dangerous, unconvenient and unsafe for the people to assemble at, for the purpose of fatiguing them into his measures, through the agency of pretended representatives; and has through his legislative council, prevented provision from being made for quiet and peaceable elections, as in the case of the late returns at Beverley.

- He has dissolved the late House of Assembly for opposing with manly firmness Sir Francis Head's invasion of the right of the people to a wholesome control over the revenue, and for insisting that the persons conducting the government should be responsible for their official conduct to the country through its representatives.

- He has endeavoured to prevent the peopling of this province and its advancement in wealth; for that purpose obstructing the laws for the naturalization of foreigners, refusing to pass others to encourage their migration hither, and raising the conditions of new appropriations of the public lands, large tracts of which he has bestowed upon unworthy persons his favorites, while deserving settlers from Germany and other countries have been used cruelly.

- He has rendered the administration of Justice liable to suspicion and distrust, by obstructing laws for establishing a fair trial by Jury, by refusing to exclude the chief criminal judge from interfering in political business, and by selecting as the judiciary violent and notorious partisans of his arbitrary power.[21]

Mackenzie's language is vivid; therefore you wish to use quotations to support your point. But as much as you would like to quote the document in full, you are writing a short essay, and a full quotation would take up too much space. For this reason, you decide to convey Mackenzie's main points by abridging his writing with marks of ellipsis:

The reformers listed a number of complaints about the ways in which King William IV treated the colony of Upper Canada. In a newspaper article most likely written by William Lyon Mackenzie they enumerated a long list of grievances including the following few: "The King of England has forbidden his governors to pass laws of immediate and pressing importance. . . . He has interfered with the freedom of elections. . . . He has dissolved the late House of Assembly. . . . He has endeavoured to prevent the peopling of this province and its advancement in wealth. . . . He has rendered the administration of Justice liable to suspicion and distrust . . ."

But notice that your sentence does not flow well into the quotation: there is a jarring difference between your verb tense and Mackenzie's. You could eliminate the problem by removing the word "has," except that you would be stuck with the incorrect form of the verb "to forbid." In addition, writing "King William" and then having the quotation repeat "he" as the subject sounds unnatural. To solve these problems, you may wish to insert some bracketed words so that your sentence flows naturally into the quotation from Mackenzie. The brackets say to your readers that these are not Mackenzie's exact words, but they still convey Mackenzie's exact meaning. You may decide to write:

In a newspaper article most likely written by Mackenzie the reformers listed a number of complaints about the ways in which King William IV treated the colony of Upper Canada, namely that he "[forbade] his governors to pass laws of immediate and pressing importance . . . interfered with the freedom of elections . . . dissolved the late House of Assembly . . . endeavoured to prevent the peopling of . . .[the] province and its advancement in wealth . . . [and] rendered the administration of justice liable to suspicion and distrust . . ."

This quotation is faithful to Mackenzie's exact meaning, even though it abridges his quotation with ellipses and brackets. It would have been unfaithful to use ellipses in the following manner: "The King of England has forbidden his governors to pass laws of immediate and pressing importance . . . for the purpose of fatiguing [the people] into his measures." This would be unfair to Mackenzie, because the first portion of the original quotation was followed by an entirely different set of ideas: "unless suspended in their operation till his assent should be obtained; and when so suspended, he has utterly neglected to attend to them."

It also would have been unfaithful to Mackenzie to use brackets in the following manner: "The King of England has forbidden his governors to pass [important] laws . . ." This changes the sense of the original quotation, "He has forbidden his governors to pass laws of immediate and pressing importance . . ." If you need to be so concise, summarizing Mackenzie in your own words would be preferable to inserting different words directly into his original writing.

Learn How to Use Quotation Marks

After apostrophes, quotation marks probably cause more confusion than any other form of punctuation. This is partly because North American practice differs from British practice. You probably read historical works from all over the English-speaking world, and when it comes to your own writing you may indeed have grounds for confusion.

1. North American Style for Quotation Marks. When you run a quotation into your text, place the words of the quotation inside double quotation marks:

Eisenhower warned against the "military-industrial complex."

For a quotation within a quotation, use single quotation marks:

In his history of the Space Age, *The Heavens and the Earth*, Walter MacDougall writes that Eisenhower feared "the assumption of inordinate power and influence by a 'military-industrial complex' and a 'scientific-technological elite.' "[22]

Notice also how the other forms of punctuation are placed in relation to the quotation marks. Periods and commas should be placed *inside* the quotation marks. If you use question marks and exclamation points, place them inside the quotation marks only when they formed part of the original quotation. If you are adding your own question marks and exclamation points after the quotation, then place them outside the quotation marks. Colons and semicolons also go outside the quotation marks.

2. British Style for Quotation Marks. The British use quotation marks in the opposite way. When a quotation is run into the text, the words of the quotation are placed in single quotation marks:

Eisenhower warned against the 'military-industrial complex'.

For a quotation within a quotation, double quotation marks are used:

In his history of the Space Age, Walter MacDougall writes that Eisenhower feared 'the assumption of inordinate power and influence by a "military-industrial complex" and a "scientific-technological elite" '.[23]

Notice also that in British usage all other punctuation marks are placed *outside* the quotation marks.

Don't Plagiarize

Historians find unfaithful quotations disturbing, but they reserve the harshest condemnation for plagiarists. In the ancient Mediterranean world, *plagiarii* were pirates who kidnapped young children, among other misdeeds.[24] When plagiarists claim someone else's ideas as their own they steal someone else's brainchild. And contrary to folk wisdom, there is no honour among thieves. Historians do not tolerate plagiarists, and universities punish them.

Cases of plagiarism happen infrequently because there is such a powerful consensus against it. It is so pleasurable to share ideas honestly and to write history faithfully that real historians should never feel an urge to plagiarize. Historians share this commitment to honesty with writers across all the disciplines.

1. Direct Plagiarism. Direct plagiarism occurs when one writer takes another writer's exact words and passes them off as his or her own. Direct plagiarism is very easy for an informed reader to spot.

2. Indirect Plagiarism. Indirect plagiarism is more difficult to recognize and it is also more insidious. Indirect plagiarism occurs when writers paraphrase someone else's work too closely. The basic structure of the sentence or paragraph is retained, and the plagiarist substitutes an occasional new word or phrase to make the writing slightly different. For example, here is an original passage taken from Colin M. Coates's article "Commemorating the Woman Warrior of New France, Madeleine de Verchères, 1696–1930." Discussing a monument to de Verchères, Coates writes:

> Gazing upon the statue . . . , no one would mistake her for a man: the swirling dress, the feminine facial features, the long braids dangling down her back, the pubescent breasts, all precluded misinterpretation. Only her (men's) hat and massive gun hinted otherwise."[25]

The following passage is an overly close paraphrase that would be an example of indirect plagiarism:

> Looking at the memorial, she could not be taken for a male. Her womanly clothes, appearance and shape would prevent mistake. Nothing but her hat and gun suggested masculinity.

This would be indirect plagiarism even if the author gave a citation to Coates. The paraphrase is too close to Coates's original text to be considered the author's original writing.

3. *Inadvertent Plagiarism*. What if you accidentally forget to put quotation marks around a passage from someone else's writing? What if you forget to provide a citation when you summarized someone else's writing? Think for a minute about your audience. When they read your work, all they see are the words in front of them. They do not see how you were frantically putting your essay together at two in the morning. By the time you tell them that you were in a rush and made some mistakes, they will not care. When your readers detect a misstep on your part, they will instinctively form the worst possible impression of you.

Recently, two popular historians, Stephen Ambrose and Doris Kearns Goodwin, have had to defend themselves against plagiarism: they have admitted to sloppy research practices. This is a common defense against charges of plagiarism. It is also an embarrassing way to defend oneself. In the case of Ambrose and Goodwin, the "sloppiness" defence highlights the relationship between plagiarism and lack of self-discipline. Historians must avoid situations that may be conducive to plagiarism. Do not wait until the last minute to research and write historical essays. Be sure that there is plenty of time to document historical sources correctly.

In history you are guilty until proven innocent. To make matters worse, it will be easy for your readers to prove your guilt, and it will be difficult for you to prove your innocence. Perhaps this is not fair, but this is how your audience thinks.

4. *Academic Dishonesty*. Plagiarism means that you are passing off someone else's work as your own. Therefore, it should go without saying that you should not submit an essay that someone else wrote for you. This includes buying a paper from a disreputable company, downloading a paper from the Internet, or submitting a paper from a fraternity file. If you do these things you are a plagiarist because someone else did your work for you. According to most university regulations, anyone who supplies you with such a paper is also a plagiarist.

There are other acts of academic dishonesty that closely resemble plagiarism. Submitting the same paper in two courses means that you are passing off work done in one course as work done in another course. Usually, dual submissions require the permission of both instructors. In addition, an instructor's permission is usually required if you want to submit a paper that you wrote in collaboration with another student. You should not pass off the other student's writing as your own writing. It is usually appropriate for you to discuss a paper assignment with another student, but when it comes to writing, do it alone.

Be Honest, but Don't Give Unnecessary Citations

It is conceivable that after reading the preceding section on plagiarism and dishonesty, you will be so frightened that you will provide a citation in every sentence you write. Don't go overboard with citations. Provide a citation when you quote directly, when you paraphrase or summarize someone else's ideas, or when you are consciously imitating the structure of someone else's writing. There is no need to provide a citation for a piece of information that reasonable people consider to be general knowledge, for example, that the Allies landed at Normandy on June 6, 1944, or that railroads played a significant role in British industrialization. These pieces of information should be obvious to everyone who has studied history. Of course, if you are unsure whether something is common knowledge, play it safe and provide a citation.[26]

Choose a Citation System That Suits Your Audience

All scholars agree to use sources responsibly. Two rules apply to all citation systems: be consistent and make it easy for your readers to check your sources. There is less agreement among scholars about specific formats for citing source materials. This is for a variety of reasons. Some publishers and editors may require special methods for citing sources, and some college instructors may have special requirements, too. For this reason it is important for historians to find out which format their audience expects them to use.

Students sometimes find citing sources to be confusing, often because history instructors have different rules from teachers in other disciplines. For example, many social scientists use a system where they place an author's name, date of publication, and page number in parentheses after a quotation, summary, or paraphrase. Sometimes historians find this system suits an essay or book particularly well. Nevertheless, most historians use sequential footnotes or endnotes.

Several guides to citations exist, but there is one guide that is widely recognized by historians: Kate L. Turabian, *A Manual for Writers of Term Papers, Theses, and Dissertations*, 6th ed. (Chicago: University of Chicago Press, 1993). "Turabian," as it is called, is a shorter version of the rules contained in the *Chicago Manual of Style*, which most historians consider to be the authoritative guide for preparing manuscripts. You will find that historians and their editors usually follow Turabian and the *Chicago Manual* in their professional publications.

Most history instructors prefer that students use footnotes or endnotes, which are easy to create in word-processing programs. The following rules apply to them. For special or unusual circumstances, refer to Turabian or the *Chicago Manual*, both of which can be found in any academic library.

1. Formatting Footnotes and Endnotes on a Word Processor.
It is usually possible to format a word-processing program to handle some aspects of noting automatically. Notes should be single-spaced in the same font size as the main text. The first line of the note may begin with an indentation from the left margin, or it may also begin with a hanging indentation. After the note number, insert a period and a space.

2. Citing a Book.   Endnotes and footnotes to books should be written like this:

> 4. W.S. MacNutt, *The Atlantic Provinces: the Emergence of Colonial Society, 1712–1867* (Toronto: McClelland and Stewart, 1965), 14–23.

Notice the following things that distinguish a footnote or endnote from a bibliographic entry: the author's first name comes first, information about the publisher is placed in parentheses, and a comma precedes the page numbers. There is usually no need for a "p." or a "pp." in front of the page numbers, unless there are grounds for confusion with other numbers in the citation.

3. Citing Different Kinds of Books.　Not all books have such simple publication information. In fact, the possible permutations are endless. Given below are some standard types of books that historical writers often cite: a multi-author book, a multi-volume book, an edited volume, and a revised edition.

11. Sally Ross and Alphonse Deveau, *The Acadians of Nova Scotia Past and Present* (Halifax: Nimbus, 1992), 73.
12. J. Murray Beck, *Joseph Howe*, 2 vols. (Kingston and Montreal: McGill-Queen's University Press, 1982), 2: 133.
13. *Farm, Factory and Fortune: New Studies in the Economic History of the Maritime Provinces*, ed. Kris Inwood (Fredericton: Acadiensis, 1993), 23–25.
14. Alan D. McMillan, *Native Peoples and Culture of Canada: an Anthropological Overview* (Vancouver and Toronto: Douglas & McIntyre, 1988; 2nd ed., 1995), 113.

4. Citing Scholarly Articles.　Scholarly articles by historians are usually published in either scholarly journals or edited collections. The form for edited collections resembles a book citation:

37. R. Ommer, "The Cod Trade of the New World," in *A People of the Sea: the Maritime History of the Channel Islands*, ed. A.G. Jamieson (London: Methuen, 1986), 251.

Journal articles are cited somewhat differently. The author and title are given, followed by the title of the journal, its volume and number, the date in parentheses, and a colon followed by the page number. Here is a simple citation and one that is more complex.

38. Janice Potter, "Patriarchy and Paternalism: the Case of the Eastern Ontario Loyalist Women," *Ontario History* 81, 1 (March 1989): 17.
39. Jane Errington, "'Woman . . . is a Very Interesting Creature': Some Women's Experiences in Early Upper Canada," *Historic Kingston*, 38 (1990): 18.

Ordinarily, an article title is simply placed in quotation marks, followed by the underlined or italicized journal title, and the publication information. Observe that in the example above, we can see special punctuation marks. In the first part of the title, there is a quotation, placed in single quotation marks within the double quotation marks. If the quotation were of a book title rather than simply a phrase, this book title would also be underlined or italicized.

5. Citing Works of Journalism. Articles in newspapers and magazines may provide less publication information than scholarly articles, but historians should still provide as much information as possible, in the following order: author, title of article, title of magazine or newspaper, date, and page number. For example,

> 40. Bob Levin and Rae Corelli, "The Tracks of History," *Maclean's*, 6 July 1992, 18.

6. Citing Unpublished Secondary Works. Sometimes you will need to provide a citation to an unpublished secondary work. It is not unusual to discover useful unpublished theses and dissertations during the course of your research, although you may need to have the author's permission to read or cite one. (Ask the librarian if you need permission.) Cite theses and dissertations according to this format:

> 8. Nanci Delayen, "The Fabian Society and Eugenics, 1885–1914" (MA thesis, University of Saskatchewan, 1998), 57.

Historians also circulate unpublished papers or manuscripts to each other. Professional courtesy dictates that these may be used and cited only when the author permits it.

> 33. William K. Storey, "Science and the Making of a British Ideology of Development in Post-Emancipation Barbados" (unpublished manuscript in the author's possession), 14.

7. Citing Interviews, Lectures, and Oral Presentations. These kinds of citations should give the name of the source and the place and date on which he or she gave you the information. Courtesy dictates that private conversations should not be cited unless you have the permission of the person you interviewed.

76. Ernest Hemingway, interview with the author, Key West, Florida, 6 September 1932.

8. Citing Archival Sources. Each archive is organized differently, but citations should be provided that will allow readers to trace your sources. Some archives, such as Britain's Public Record Office (PRO), even provide readers with standard guidelines for citing sources from their collection. The following source was found in the PRO, in the Colonial Office (CO) files labeled number 167:

61. Lees to Knutsford, with minutes by Wingfield, 9 Jan. 1891, PRO CO 167/661.

If you are conducting research in an archive, be sure to ask if there is a correct way to cite their sources. If not, be sure that your readers understand any abbreviations you may choose to use.

9. Citing the Internet. Standards for citing sources on the Internet have not yet evolved completely. Even so, Internet citations follow the same principles as other citations: they should give readers all the information they need to find a source. Internet citations should give the full Universal Resource Locator (URL) address of the source, not just the homepage.

As much as it is important to follow the same principles as with other citations, it is also important to acknowledge that Internet citations are different from print sources. Print sources are usually permanent; they can almost always be located in a major research library. Internet sites may change or disappear.

There are several ways in which historical citations can address the Internet's impermanence. A citation should always give the date of publication and also the date of retrieval. That way, readers will know that you saw content that was available at that time. Should a reader challenge your use of a source, it will be helpful for you to have a printout of the Internet site from the day on which you used it.

There are also minor ways in which the Internet is different for purposes of citation. First you may give conventional citation information, such as author, title, and date of publication. But then you must also give an Internet address, and some Internet sites have addresses that are long and unattractive. Historians have taken to placing Internet addresses in angle brackets, like these: < >. Follow the Internet address with the date on which you retrieved the information placed in regular parentheses, like these: ( ). Let us now take a look at a well-known historical website, *Who Killed William Robinson?*, written by Ruth Sandwell and John Lutz. This website contains reproductions of many primary and secondary sources, including photographs, newspaper articles, legal documents, correspondence, diaries, artists' reconstructions, paintings, and historians' commentaries, all pertaining to a nineteenth-century murder case on Saltspring Island in British Columbia. When citing a newspaper article from *Who Killed William Robinson?*, use the following method:

> 42. "Threats," *British Colonist*, 3 June, 1869. *Who Killed William Robinson?*, <http://web.uvic.ca/history-robinson/indexmsn. html > (17 Aug. 2003).

If you know the newspaper page and column number, include it after the publication date. Note that in this case the website provides only one main address, as shown on its homepage. Some sites show individual addresses for each section or document, so be sure to check carefully for these and to include them where appropriate.

10. How to Repeat a Citation Without Using Latin Abbreviations.   In the olden days, when historians wanted to cite a work for the second time, they used "ibid." if the citation followed the original citation immediately, and they used "op. cit." and "loc. cit." when the citation came after citations to other works.

No more! The *Chicago Manual* now considers op. cit. and loc. cit. to be archaic and obsolete. Ibid. may still be used, but when you revise an essay by cutting and pasting paragraphs, you may find that using ibid. in your notes will make it difficult to keep track of your sources. There is an easier, simpler system for shortening references. The first time you cite a source, give the full citation, but after the first time give an abbreviation: author's last name, abbreviated title, and page number. Here are some examples:

> 11. Denis Judd, *Empire: The British Imperial Experience from 1765 to the Present* (New York: Basic Books, 1996), 79.

12. Judd, *Empire*, 80.
13. Bruno Latour, *We Have Never Been Modern*, trans. Catherine Porter (Cambridge: Harvard University Press, 1993), 90.
14. Latour, *Never Been Modern*, 91.
15. Judd, *Empire*, 84.
16. Latour, *Never Been Modern*, 91.

11. How to Place a Superscript Note in the Main Text.   When you read, notice that most historians place a note at the end of a sentence, not in the middle. Notes in the middle of a sentence are annoying and distracting. They should be used only when they are absolutely necessary to distinguish one person's ideas from another. Here is an example of a poorly placed note: "J.R. Miller argues[4] that the First Nations peoples in Canada constantly attempted to determine their own paths, rather than simply accept the dictates of Euro-Canadians." The note number really belongs at the end of the sentence, because at that point you are still discussing Miller and his book *Skyscrapers Hide the Heavens* (Toronto: University of Toronto Press, 1989). The only way that it would be appropriate to place the number in the middle of the sentence would be if you had to distinguish Miller's ideas from someone else's: "Miller argues that the First Nations peoples in Canada constantly attempted to determine their own paths, rather than simply accepting the dictates of Euro-Canadians,[4] but other writers feel differently."

12. Citing a Quotation of a Quotation.   Historians prefer to quote from original sources. If you see a primary source quotation in a secondary work and you want to quote it yourself, check the primary source and assess the accuracy of the quotation. When you go back and find the original primary source, this entitles you to cite the primary source.

Sometimes it may not be possible for you to find the original primary source. In this case, acknowledge the primary source but say "as cited in" or "as quoted by" the secondary work. Imagine that you are reading about the execution of Louis XVI in Simon Schama's book, *Citizens: A Chronicle of the French Revolution*. Schama describes the scene, in part, by quoting from a memoir by Louis-Sébastien Mercier:

His blood flowed and cries of joy from eighty thousand armed men struck my ears. . . . I saw the schoolboys of the Quatre-

Nations throw their hats in the air; his blood flowed and some dipped their fingers in it, or a pen or a piece of paper; one tasted it and said *Il est bougrement salé* . . .

You may wish to use this colourful quotation in your own work, but unless you have access to a very large university library, you may have difficulty tracking down the original source. You are still welcome to use the quotation if you attribute the quotation in a citation that follows this format:

> 27. Louis-Sébastien Mercier, as cited in Simon Schama, *Citizens: A Chronicle of the French Revolution* (New York: Knopf, 1989), 670.

13. Discursive Notes.   When you read works of history, you will notice that some authors use endnotes or footnotes to introduce and clarify points of interpretation, or even to take digressions from their subjects. These discursive notes may be fine from the author's point of view, but readers often find them annoying. If something is important enough to say, why not say it in the main body of the text? Discursive footnotes should be restricted to comments about difficulties readers might have in locating or interpreting source materials.

14. Know the Difference Between Note Format and Bibliographic Format.   Sometimes you will need to add a bibliography to an essay, especially if it is a long one. If you have been using footnotes or endnotes, the following bibliographic format is appropriate for books: the author's last name comes first because bibliographies are alphabetized; a period comes after the author's name and after the title; and there are no parentheses around the publication information. With articles, add the full number of pages after the final colon. Bibliographies also usually have a hanging indent, meaning that the first line of an entry is five spaces to the left of the following lines:

Harney, Robert F. "Montreal's King of Italian Labour: A Case Study of Padronism," *Labour/Le Travailleur* 4(1979): 57–84.

Iacovetta, Franca. *Such Hardworking People: Italian Immigrants in Postwar Toronto*. Montreal: McGill-Queen's University Press, 1992.

For further questions about bibliographies and citations, see either Turabian or the *Chicago Manual*. These are the authoritative guides for historians.

In addition to providing guidance on footnotes and endnotes, these guides will also provide advice on alternative styles of citation that are used less frequently in research-based historical essays. These include the Modern Language Association (MLA) style of in-text citation, commonly used in literature, and the American Psychological Association (APA) style of in-text citation, commonly used in the social sciences. Note that the fifth edition of the MLA Handbook includes an appendix section on endnotes and footnotes.

⚛ 4 ⚛

USE SOURCES TO
MAKE INFERENCES

It is impossible to know exactly what happened in the past, but that has not stopped people from writing about it. Walt Whitman wrote in *Specimen Days* that the "interior history" of the American Civil War "will not only never be written—its practicality, minutiae of deeds and passions, will never be even suggested."[27] That may be so, but Whitman still tried to interpret the Civil War. He did so by making reasoned inferences from his sources.

An inference is more than just a hunch. It is an intelligent conclusion based on the examination and comparison of evidence. When Whitman examined the wounded soldiers in a Washington, DC, army hospital, he concluded that the Civil War was indescribably brutal. Whitman wrote this about the war, and people believed him, even though the poet had not seen every casualty and every battlefield. He had seen enough wounded men to build his inference into a persuasive argument. Like Whitman, historians also suggest probable interpretations by using their sources to make inferences.

What is it, then, that makes an inferential argument interesting? Good writers make inferences by juxtaposing sources in a new, provocative way. Whitman recognized that during the Civil War not everyone wanted to hear a message from a pacifist. People on both sides were mobilizing armies to kill and maim each other, without fully considering the evidence that Whitman saw in the army hospital. Whitman hoped that his evidence, built by inferences into an argument, might change the way people thought about the war. New evidence, or a new approach to old evidence, called into question the received wisdom of the day.

Inferential reasoning is based on thoughtful comparison. When modern-day historians write about the past, they assess source materials by cross-checking information. Historians never read sources alone. Even when historians have just one source on a given subject, they will read it in the context of their own general knowledge, and they will try as hard as they can to compare a source with other works.

Be True to Recognized Facts

All inferences begin with a consideration of the facts. Some facts are easy to recognize, but occasionally you may encounter people who are unduly skeptical about recognized facts. Some polemicists posing as historians make extravagant claims about facts. Millions of people witnessed, documented, and experienced the Holocaust, but there is an organization that denies that the Holocaust ever happened. It even has its own journal dedicated to "proving" its point.[28] Real historical writers probe factual uncertainties but they do not invent convenient facts and they do not ignore inconvenient facts. People are entitled to their own opinions, but not to their own facts.

Transform Facts into Evidence

Facts do not just exist by themselves and conveniently prove things. Historical writers do not just collect facts, they make inferences from them. There is more to writing history than simply gathering facts like the detectives on Dragnet. ("Just the facts, ma'am, just the facts.") Even on television crime dramas, facts are examined and interpreted in the courtroom. Like "expert witnesses," historians determine the authenticity of factual information. They select only the most reliable and informative facts, and they use only these to make inferences.

Check Your Facts

Sometimes the facts are not what they seem, and it is not always easy to discern where "the facts" stop and interpretation starts. At the end of the 1960s many professional historians believed that European ships delivered at least 15 million African slaves to the New World. How did these figures become a fact? Philip Curtin suspected that the figure was erroneous. He checked a chain of misguided citations and discovered that the figure of 15 million rested upon the speculations of an obscure American pamphleteer who wrote during the 1850s. Curtin inferred from these miscalculations that it would be useful for a modern-day historian to count the number of slaves anew. He conducted his own research, which he published in *The Atlantic Slave Trade: A Census*. In this book, Curtin estimated that 9.5 million slaves were imported.[29] Historians should follow Curtin's example and take an informed but pragmatic approach to facts. Most often facts will be self-evident, but sometimes historians find that facts rest on nothing more than received wisdom. Historical writers must check their sources. Be aware of the processes for establishing things as factual.

Check the Internal Consistency of Primary Sources

A document will not often contradict itself, and if it does, there might be a reason. For example, the richest sources for rural north China in the early twentieth century are the written reports of the Japanese government's South Manchurian Railway Company from 1940 to 1942. These reports contain many contradictions, for a good reason: during the Japanese occupation, the company sent teams of sociologists to interview large numbers of villagers. Not surprisingly, the peasants of occupied China mistrusted the occupiers, and sometimes they lied to them. Even so, several historians have used the interviews as sources to reconstruct the economy, society, and politics of the region.[30] Historians have done this through the use of internal inferences, in other words, by comparing discrete parts of the sources with each other. Individual peasants may have lied to the Japanese on specific issues, meaning that all their statements must be checked against each other. These records can still reveal a great deal when used skeptically and responsibly, but historians have not stopped there: they have used them in light of other sources about rural north China, too. All sources have been subject to some biases in creation and selection, but that does not mean that historians cannot try to determine what happened.

Check Primary Sources Against Each Other

Comparing source materials can lead to important new inferences. To illustrate such a breakthrough inference, it is instructive to examine the well-known life of Louis Pasteur, who made some of the most significant contributions to nineteenth-century biology. After Pasteur died in 1895, his colleagues, admirers, and relatives published chronicles of his life. Historians used these sources skeptically, but they had few alternative accounts that were critical of Pasteur. One of the only critical accounts was written by Pasteur's nephew and laboratory assistant, Adrien Loir. He intimated that at the public trials of the anthrax vaccine, Pasteur misled the judges. However, Loir presented little evidence to support his claim, so most historians continued to trust the positive accounts of Pasteur's supporters. But recently, Gerald Geison became the first historian to gain access to Pasteur's laboratory notebooks. When he read them, he found that they confirmed Loir's account. Geison then used the notebooks to reevaluate Pasteur's experimental practices, leading him to move Loir's account from the background to the foreground. A simple comparison of sources made it possible to make a significant inference about Pasteur, which provided Geison with a motive to write a book, *The Private Science of Louis Pasteur*.[31]

Compare Primary Sources with Secondary Works

Historical knowledge changes incrementally as new interpretations of primary sources alter historians' understanding of the past. Historians often find themselves using primary sources to refine or contradict the ideas that other historians present in secondary works. One recent example comes from the field of environmental history. In Guinée in West Africa, numerous patches of forest can be seen in the grasslands surrounding Kissidougou. From the 1890s until the

1990s, European scientists visited the area. They believed it was a fact that the local inhabitants were converting forest to grassland; the patches of trees were obviously remnants of old forests. They wrote up their opinions in secondary works about the forests. It was only in the 1990s that two outside historians, James Fairhead and Melissa Leach, took the trouble to interview the local people and ask them to explain the patches of trees. They learned some surprising information: for all these years, the villagers had been planting the forest patches in the grasslands. The European scientists had been reading the history of the landscape backwards. The interviews were a primary source that forced a fundamental reconsideration of the secondary works. In their book, *Misreading the African Landscape*, Fairhead and Leach showed what every good historical writer knows: that historians must cast a skeptical eye on their sources.[32]

Fairhead and Leach uncovered a primary source that called into question a secondary work. The reverse is possible, too. Historian Jan Vansina used a familiar body of secondary works to find a way to look at some new and unfamiliar primary sources. In 1953, Vansina was visiting the Congo for the first time. He had been studying medieval European history, and he had even written his master's thesis on Latin funerary dirges. He knew a lot about the historical literature on medieval Europe, but very little about African history, a subject that few Europeans studied in those days. Vansina met a Kuba village historian named Mbop Louis who told him, "We too know the past, because we carry our newspapers in our heads." Mbop recited a historical poem, which Vansina thought resembled one of the Latin dirges he knew so well. He used his knowledge of medievalist scholarship to formulate an approach to this oral primary source.[33] Vansina went on to write some of the pioneering works in African history, based on his insight that all sources could be compared, no matter how unusual the comparison might be.

Conduct Interviews Systematically

Interviewing people can be one of the most exciting aspects of historical research. When you are working on a history, an interview can bring a sense of immediacy to the research and the writing. But an interview is more than just a conversation: it is a way to seek critical information about the past. Be as systematic as possible in your interviewing. Here are some guidelines:

1. **Do your homework.** Before you conduct the interview, learn what you can from written sources. Then make a list of questions that you want to ask your subject. If you do not know some basic information about your history, you will waste your time and your subject's. Your subject will also think that you do not know what you are talking about and will not trust you.

2. **Be considerate.** Tell your subjects about your project and ask for permission to quote. They may only be willing to share information with you anonymously. *You must respect their wishes because their position may be more delicate than you think.* If you are a student, your college or university may also have published ethical guidelines for conducting research with other people as subjects. Ask your instructor if this is the case, and be sure to follow the guidelines. If you are a graduate student, a postdoctoral researcher, or a faculty member, you will almost certainly be obliged to follow your university's standards for research on "human subjects." Useful guidelines have also been published by the American Historical Association, in their "Statement on Interviewing for Historical Documentation," which can be found by clicking on <http://www.theaha.org/pubs/standard.htm>, and then clicking on the title. All warnings aside, you will find that many people enjoy being interviewed for a history: it can be very flattering to know that one's work has been historically significant.

3. **Be patient.** It takes time to interview people, and it may even be difficult to get in touch with some subjects. Often you will find that it is a good idea to have references, or even to mail your potential subject a resumé and a brief description of your project. It might also take two or three interviews before your subject trusts you enough to share interesting information with you. If you plan to interview people, start work early so that you can meet your deadlines.

4. **Take scrupulous notes.** Always take written notes during an interview. You may also want to use a tape

recorder, but batteries can die and the wrong buttons can get pressed. Back up your work with written notes. Technical problems happen, but they are not the only problems with tape-recorded notes. A tape recording gives you a more accurate record of the interview, but it can also frighten your subjects. If you notice that the tape recorder is interfering with the interview, shut it off.

5. **Think critically about oral sources.** Interviews are often reliable, but they should be subject to critical evaluation. Be aware that your subjects may not remember events exactly as they happened. If it is possible, compare their stories with the stories that other people tell you, and also compare oral sources with any available written sources. Written sources are not necessarily more reliable than oral sources, but writing can often be a more effective way to preserve a version of history.

6. **Cultivate your skills as an interviewer and as an interpreter of interviews.** It takes a lot of practice to learn how to work with sources, and interviewing is no different. The best interviewers are usually the most experienced. There are also a number of good guides to interviewing. For an informal introduction, see Richard Rhodes, *How to Write: Advice and Reflections* (New York: Quill, 1995), 72 to 75. For a formal introduction to interviewing and other aspects of working "in the field," see Robert M. Emerson, *Writing Ethnographic Fieldnotes* (Chicago: University of Chicago Press, 1995). For a discussion of how to interpret oral testimony, see Jan Vansina, *Oral Tradition as History* (Madison: University of Wisconsin Press, 1985). For a contrasting view, see David William Cohen, *The Combing of History* (Chicago: University of Chicago Press, 1994).

Juxtapose Sources to Make Inferences

During the course of your research and writing, you will be constantly reading sources in the context of other sources. You will need to check primary sources and secondary works for internal consistency. You will also need to compare primary sources and secondary works against each other. How might all this advice work together in practice? Imagine that you are beginning with a primary source, a song by Robert Johnson of the Mississippi Delta called "Crossroads Blues," recorded in the 1930s:

> I went down to the crossroads,
> Fell down on my knees.
> I went down to the crossroads,
> Fell down on my knees.
> Ask the lord above for mercy,
> Say boy, if you please.

What can historians tell from only the text of this song? The singer goes to the crossroads to pray, and even as he asks God for mercy, he employs a somewhat irreverent tone. Historians know that Johnson sang it in the Delta, but the song itself does not seem to make any particular reference to the place. Standing by itself, this song may not be very interesting, at least from a historical standpoint.

The "Crossroads Blues" might only refer to praying, but historians might be able to gain a better understanding of the song if they knew something about Robert Johnson. In a book called *Standing at the Crossroads*, historian Pete Daniel writes that as a young man, Johnson knew the blues artists Son House, Willie Brown, and Charley Patton. During the 1920s, all of them worked and played in the vicinity of the Dockery plantation in the Mississippi Delta. Johnson could not play as well as the others, and at one point he simply disappeared, seemingly leaving for good. But several months later Johnson reappeared, and he had become a much better guitar player. The legend developed that Johnson had gone down to the crossroads and sold his soul to the Devil so that he could play the blues. This legend casts some light on how Johnson's audience understood the song.[34] Historians might reasonably make the inference that Johnson played the song to perpetuate a legend among his audience.

Pete Daniel makes it possible to interpret the "Crossroads Blues" in the context of the legends surrounding Johnson's life, but it might be possible to make some further inferences about the song from some other comparisons. The references to the Devil are fascinating, and it might be possible to find a source that would place Johnson's song in the context of African-American religious practices. In a history of the Delta called *The Most Southern Place on Earth*, James Cobb argues that blues musicians, like other African Americans, had a different concept of the Devil from European Americans. The Devil was not a sinister Satan but a playful trickster who resembled the African god Legba. When Johnson associated himself with the Devil, he was advertising himself as dangerous, but not as European Americans might conventionally understand it.[35]

Is there any validity to this position? Could Robert Johnson's song have anything to do with African religious practices that were retained in African-American culture? Tracing a few footnotes makes it possible to draw further inferences from textual comparisons. Several essays in a collection edited by Joseph Holloway, *Africanisms in American Culture*, substantiate the case that African religious and musical practices were indeed retained and developed in African-American culture. One essay by Robert Farris Thompson shows plenty of evidence to suggest that crosses and crossroads were considered to be sacred by the Kongo people, and that these symbols remained important in African-American art and folklore. Another essay, by Margaret Washington Creel, tells more about the significance of the cross in Kongo religious practices. Archaeological evidence and oral histories suggest that the cross was a symbol in Kongo religion long before the introduction of Christianity to the region, and that during the Christian era Kongo ideas about religion can be found in coastal Georgia and South Carolina.[36] When read in the context of this information, Robert Johnson's song becomes a significant piece of evidence for building the case that some elements of African culture survived the experience of slavery.

Creel supports her argument partly by making reference to John Janzen and Wyatt MacGaffey, who published a collection of Kongo oral histories during the 1970s. One of MacGaffey's recorded texts is particularly interesting to compare with the "Crossroads Blues." In it, a man named Kingani describes how he went to the crossroads and prayed to the spirits of his ancestors for the health of his child.[37] This Kongo text bears an obvious resemblance to Robert Johnson's song. Such a comparison does not show that Johnson was necessarily conscious of African religious traditions. It does suggest the inference that Johnson may have been drawing on a folk tradition that had its origins on the other side of the Atlantic. Making such inferences by comparisons can make it easier to appreciate any discrete piece of evidence.

Make Inferences from Material Sources

Most academic writers analyze written source materials. Therefore, it takes some practice for historians to learn how to approach objects as sources. But many historians, including historians of science and technology, archaeologists, and art historians, do work frequently with objects. Learning to analyze objects can give you new perspectives on things, but it is not easy to learn how. Try to follow these guidelines, which are borrowed from an article by Jules Prown called "Mind in Matter." These are common methods used by writers across the disciplines to analyze materials.

1. **Describe the object.** What can you observe in the object itself? Give a physical description of the object. How is it shaped? If you can measure it, what are its dimensions (size, weight)? If you cannot measure it, estimate the dimensions. Can you find any obvious symbols on the object, such as markings, decorations, or inscriptions?

2. **Thinking about the object.** At this very moment, what is it like to interact with the object? What does the object feel like? When you use the object, do you have to take into account its size, weight, or shape? What does the object do, and how does it do it? Does it work well? What is it like to use it? How do you feel about using this object? Do you like it? Does it frustrate you? Is it puzzling?

3. **Making an argument about the object.** Can you analyze the object imaginatively and plausibly? Review your descriptions and deductions. What sorts of hypotheses can you make about the object? Can you make a historically significant argument about the object? What might it have been like for someone to use this object in the past? Use other sources as a lens for interpreting the object. What other evidence can you use to test your hypotheses, speculations, and deductions?[38]

Move from Inferences to Arguments

The process of making inferences allows historians to say some-thing new. This can be an intimidating proposition, especially if you are working on a topic that has been studied extensively. But judging by the contents of most bookstores, historians are always finding something new to say about old topics. Just when you think the Second World War has been studied to death, a new book ap-pears.

There are many ways to say something new. Experienced his-torians know that new ideas come out of close and careful compar-isons of primary sources and secondary works. A new idea in one field can shed light on an old source; the discovery of a new source can inspire historians to rethink some old ideas. In fact, every indi-vidual historian brings a unique personal perspective to all sources.

Still, novelty is not enough and novelty for its own sake is not useful. Small inferences must be built into larger arguments, and arguments must be made persuasively. When you read your sources, start thinking about ways to compose your essay. How can you move from asking questions about events and sources to composing a story and an argument of your own? This is the most challenging aspect to writing any history. You must consider the arguments of your primary sources and secondary works, then engage them con-structively and responsibly.

Make Reasonable Inferences from Your Sources

Source materials impose healthy constraints on historical writers. You may have a hunch that space aliens helped the Egyptians to build the pyramids, but after careful review of primary sources and secondary works, you will find no evidence to support your hypoth-esis. Don't worry. You thought that you could make a breathtak-ingly novel argument, but it is much more important that you rec-ognize the limits of your sources. Do not expect too much from your sources, and do not read into them what you hope to find. Some-times you can even write an essay about how little you can tell from the sources. Even so, if you cannot use a source to support your argument, you must be prepared to either redefine your questions or move on to another set of sources.

Make Inferences That Are Warranted

Some inferences are better than others, but how do historians know what makes a good inference? Historians must have a reason to believe an inference. For this reason, it is important to try to answer the following question: under which circumstances are inferences warranted?

The ancient Greeks divided arguments from inferences into two categories: deduction and induction. When you are reading and writing history, use the categories of deduction and induction to help you decide which arguments from inferences are warranted.

1. Deductive Reasoning. In deductive reasoning, a writer makes an inference based on a limited amount of evidence, but the inference is still trustworthy because it is consonant with conventional wisdom. In other words, deduction means that we are applying general rules to particular circumstances.

Writers understand deductions by breaking deductive warrants down into their stated and unstated components. Here is an example of a historical deduction: "The gaps in the Watergate tapes must mean that Nixon was trying to hide something." What sort of evidence do historians have to support this statement? The Watergate tapes do contain large gaps, but Nixon never admitted to hiding anything—he said that his secretary accidentally erased portions of the tapes. Why didn't anybody believe Nixon? Common sense indicates that Nixon erased key, incriminating passages from the tapes. Most people would argue that Nixon had a motive, and he also had access.

Break this argument down into its deductive components, and this is what it looks like:

- Evidence: The Watergate tapes contain large gaps.
- Commonsense warrant: People erase tapes in order to destroy information.
- Inference: When Nixon delivered the incomplete Watergate tapes to investigators, he must have been hiding something.

Usually writers do not state their reasoning in such a schematic way, but a commonsense deduction can provide a warrant for believing an inference based on a limited source.

In some cases common sense is obvious, but sometimes it is deceptive. It is possible to challenge the inferences of historical writers by testing whether their warrants really are based on common sense. All historians have heard the story about how Columbus wanted to prove that the Earth was round and not flat. According to the legend, Columbus's contemporaries believed the Earth was flat because they had a weak commonsense warrant:

- Evidence: The Earth appears to be flat.

- Commonsense warrant: People can distinguish between flat objects and round objects.

- Inference: The Earth is flat, not round.

Obviously, people may not actually be able to distinguish flat objects from round objects, at least not on the planetary scale. If your commonsense warrant does not make sense, then there must be a flaw in your reasoning. Take care to test your warrants, especially if they are unstated. If you don't test your own warrants, your audience surely will.

2. Inductive Reasoning.   Historians commonly associate inductive reasoning with scientific methods. This is because inductive reasoning begins with many particular bits of evidence and generalizes from them. During your reading and research you may observe many facts, perceive relationships between them, and draw conclusions about them.

Induction operates on the following warrant: that plenty of data can help historians to reach likely conclusions. Take the following statement: "Statistics Canada data suggest that between 1973 and 1998 wealth in Canada was increasingly concentrated into the hands of the rich." What are the components of this inductive statement?

- Evidence: Statistics Canada data shows that the gap between the incomes of the richest and poorest families in Canada widened considerably between 1973 and 1998.

- Inductive warrant: Plenty of data help people to reach likely conclusions.
- Inference: Based on the evidence, Canadian wealth was increasingly concentrated into the hands of the rich.

The most common way to test such an inference is to question whether the evidence is sufficient. The underlying inductive warrant is difficult to challenge.

Avoid Unwarranted Comparisons

Comparisons lie at the heart of historical reasoning, so be careful when you make them. Some comparisons help historians to make strong inferences about the past; other comparisons are pointless or even irresponsible. In a book called *The Unmasterable Past*, Charles Maier writes about how German historians have interpreted Nazism and the Holocaust. While surveying his topic, Maier makes the point that some historical comparisons are "licit" and some are not. The Holocaust will probably always be understood in the context of other genocides and acts of brutality, but Maier criticizes those historians who compare the Holocaust to other genocides because they want to alleviate German guilt.[39] Historians must use comparisons to build inferences that are appropriate.

Avoid Anachronistic Inferences

When historians write history they speak on behalf of people who lived in the past. This is a tremendous responsibility and challenge, which is the reason why anachronistic interpretations have no place in historical writing. Historians can bring latter-day interpretations to bear on their subjects, but historians cannot place their subjects in situations they would never recognize.

Some anachronisms are easy to avoid. No sensible person would ever write this sentence: "Just before Caesar crossed the Rubicon, he glanced at his wristwatch and wondered if it would ever be time for tea." Obviously, Caesar did not have a wristwatch or tea. Even so, anachronisms often present problems that are more subtle. For example, historian Georges Lefebvre wanted to use Marxist theory to explain the origins of the French Revolution. But when Lefebvre wrote the book *The Coming of the French Revolution*, he knew he could not argue that the French working classes intended to form a communist party and establish a dictatorship of the proletariat. Such an anachronistic claim would not have been true to the experience of eighteenth-century French people, who had never heard of such things as the communist party or the dictatorship of the proletariat. Instead, Lefebvre gained a heightened awareness of class conflict from reading Marx, then used this awareness to ask new questions of his sources.[40]

Many students get interested in history because they want to explain the origins of contemporary problems. This is a common way to ask questions about the past, but historians must also respect the outlook of people who lived in the past. For example, historians may see the origins of modern physics in Newton's *Principia*, but Newton must be understood in the context of the seventeenth century. Like many of his contemporaries, Newton had interests in alchemy and religion that bear little relation to modern physics and that may seem bizarre and even foolish from a modern perspective. As Betty Jo Teeter Dobbs shows in her book, *The Janus Face of Genius*, it is important for a historian to understand Newton's own perspective and to ask how his understanding of mechanics related to his understanding of alchemy and religion.[41] The power of hindsight makes it perfectly legitimate for historical writers to ask contemporary questions about old materials, but historians must remain faithful to the perspective of the people who lived through the times under study.

⊰ 5 ⊱

GET WRITING!

After spending days, weeks, or months gathering and analyzing information, the time will come when you have to start writing. Making the transition from research to writing is often the most difficult stage of a project, but it must be done. Scholars facing the blank computer screen would do well to heed the advice of Samuel Eliot Morison, one of the greatest historians of navigation. In an article called "History as a Literary Art: An Appeal to Young Historians," Morison advised students to avoid the temptations to find that one last source or to brew another pot of coffee. Instead of procrastinating, Morison insisted that his students should "First and foremost, *get writing!*"[42] Once you start to write, you will have to think more rigorously about what it is that you want to say.

Consider Narratives and Analysis

Morison wrote, "get writing!" but how, exactly, should you start? You need to find a suitable framework for your argument, so think about how you want to organize your writing.

By now, your hypothesis has become a thesis, which is the main argument that you wish to sustain throughout your essay. You should also know which pieces of evidence you will be using to support your main argument. But chances are that you do not know yet whether you will organize the essay as one long narrative that touches on analytical topics, or as an analysis that uses short narratives to illustrate specific points.

Create a Draft Outline of an Analytical Essay

In the early stages of writing, it is usually a good idea to make an outline of your essay. Here you will merely sketch out the broader organization of an essay in order to test its feasibility.

If you are still writing a paper on the history of longitude, a draft outline of an analytical essay might look something like this:

    I. Introduction: science, culture, and longitude
   II. John Harrison
       A. His background
       B. His inventions
       C. The chronometer trials
  III. Nevil Maskelyne
       A. His background
       B. His inventions
       C. His bias against Harrison
   IV. Conclusion
       A. George III decides the case
       B. Significance of the case

This is an analytical essay because it is organized around an analytical point: the relationship between science and culture. It does not tell one narrative, but it compares several narratives: the story of Harrison and the story of Maskelyne; the story of how Maskelyne tested Harrison's clocks and the story of how George III tested them. This organization highlights an analytical problem—in this case, whether scientists are biased.

Create a Draft Outline of a Narrative Essay

It is also possible to organize your longitude essay around one narrative. In this case, you may have enough information about John Harrison to use his life's story as a narrative that contains within it important analytical points. Here is a possible draft outline of a narrative essay:

    I. Harrison's youth
       A. Education and training
       B. Becomes aware of longitude problem

II. Harrison's early solutions to the longitude problem
   A. Builds the clock H-1
   B. Builds the clock H-2
   C. Builds the clock H-3
   D. Builds the clock H-4
III. Harrison at the end of his life
   A. Wins the longitude prize
   B. Harrison dies

Complete Your Analytical Outline

The draft outlines above only provide skeletal frameworks for either an analytical essay or a narrative essay. They may be useful as beginnings, but they do not do much to help you articulate your argument. If you want a complete outline of your analytical essay, add some flesh to the bones. A complete outline of an analytical essay would explain why you are moving from one analytical topic to another.

I. Introduction: The struggle to find a solution to the longitude problem shows that science is influenced by culture. This topic is significant for two reasons:
   A. Finding longitude was a significant problem in the eighteenth century. We know this from the story of Anson's voyage of 1741.
   B. A number of social scientists are now arguing that culture influences science, and we can use this case to test their position.
II. John Harrison produced four marine chronometers, each of which met the criteria for winning the longitude prize.
   A. Brief discussion of the role of artisans in eighteenth-century London's economy and society, with brief biographical narrative about John Harrison.
   B. Tell the narrative of how Harrison built his clocks, H-1, H-2, H-3, and H-4, all of which solved the longitude problem because they embodied new mechanical innovations in clockmaking.
   C. Tell the narrative of how Harrison had difficulty persuading the judges on the Board of Longitude to believe

that he had solved the longitude problem, even though his chronometers worked.

III. The members of the Board were mostly well-educated astronomers, in other words, they were from a culture that was different from Harrison's.

A. Discuss the role of astronomers in the intellectual life of eighteenth-century England, with specific reference to universities and government.

B. Tell the narrative of how the astronomer Maskelyne had solved the longitude problem in a different way, by creating cumbersome tables that ships' captains could use to measure the distances from the moon to the planets and stars.

C. Tell the narrative of how Maskelyne's behaviour toward Harrison during the trials of the clocks illustrates his cultural bias against Harrison.

IV. Conclusion: Harrison triumphed in spite of cultural obstacles.

A. George III intervened on Harrison's behalf and recognized the superiority of Harrison's chronometers.

B. Culture may be so deeply implicated in scientific and technological research that at times it seems that inventors and scientists have to be very lucky to gain recognition.

This outline provides a core description of an analytical essay about John Harrison's solution of the longitude question. It is organized around analytical points, but it contains evidence as well as small narratives.

Complete Your Narrative Outline

Alternatively, you may wish to write a narrative of the life of John Harrison that touches on analytical issues such as the relationship between culture and science. For this essay, too, a full outline would be helpful:

I. Harrison's youth: humble origins in Yorkshire and Lincolnshire, son of a carpenter. Touch on analytical point of the place of such a family in English society.

A. As a child, Harrison learned skilled trades such as carpentry, also taught himself rudimentary mathematics and physics, unusual for someone from his background.
B. Harrison built his first pendulum clock, incorporating new technical innovations.
C. Harrison probably began to hear of problems associated with calculating longitude, a significant problem in eighteenth-century England.
II. Harrison's career as a clockmaker in London. Touch on analytical point of role of social status of artisans in London.
A. Harrison built the first marine chronometer, H-1, and during the trials had his first encounters with naval officers and astronomers. Pause to analyze how Harrison was from a different sort of class and culture from the naval officers and astronomers.
B. Harrison built H-2 and H-3, solved numerous technical problems, began to have a poor relationship with the astronomers, especially Maskelyne. Provide some social and educational background on Maskelyne.
C. Harrison built H-4, a totally new design for a marine chronometer that deserved to win the longitude prize. Harrison had serious clashes with Maskelyne during the trials, illustrating the analytical point about the relations between science and culture.
III. The end of Harrison's life
A. Harrison dissatisfied by his treatment at the hands of the Board of Longitude.
B. George III intervened on Harrison's behalf and Harrison won the prize.
C. Harrison died. End with a reflection on the significance of his life for understanding the relations between science and culture.

Choose a Framework for Your Essay

Now that you have explored how to organize your essay around analysis and narrative, it is time to choose the right framework. You must think about several questions. Which framework is best suited to your sources? Which framework will be most enjoyable to use? Which framework does your audience expect?

⊰ 6 ⊱

BUILD AN ARGUMENT

It is not enough that a historical essay should have an introduction, a series of paragraphs with evidence, and a conclusion. A good historical essay leads its readers in some direction, but it should also be said that it is challenging for a writer to articulate and sustain this direction. This is why it is crucial for an essay to have an argument. An argument is not an angry display of vituperation; it is an idea that develops over the course of an essay. An argument must capture and hold an audience's attention.

Start to Write a First Draft

The complete outlines given above contain frameworks for sustained arguments. A good outline shows the main argument as well as its significance, and it shows how subsequent sections of the argument are related to the main argument. And yet it does not really prove anything. It is, after all, only an outline.

As you think about the overall outline, go to the sources, find support for your possible arguments, and compose paragraphs around them. It is fine to start composing paragraphs that will fall in the middle of the essay, not in the beginning. An introduction does not have to be written first; in fact, you may wish to write the body of the text first. As you grapple with writing about your sources, you will discover new things about them, things that will make an early version of the introduction obsolete by the time you finish the body of the text.

While you are writing a first draft, keep in mind your argument and think about how it is evolving. As you add more analysis and information, stand back occasionally to check and see whether your argument is developing in a reasonable and interesting way. You may even find yourself changing your line of argument to the point where it does not even resemble your original argument any more. If this is so, you must return to the beginning and check the entire argument for consistency.

Grab Your Reader's Attention, but Do It Gently

Every reader asks, "Why should I read this?" "Why should I care?" Writers must give their audiences reasons to care. Many historians use the beginning of an essay or book to connect their scholarly interests to broader academic and political debates. For example, in a book called *Holy Feast and Holy Fast*, which is about medieval religious women, Caroline Walker Bynum begins with a quick discussion of the scholarship in her field. Then she grabs the reader's attention:

> Sex and money . . . again and again modern scholars have emphasized the guilt engendered by their seductiveness, the awesome heroism required for their renunciation. Yet this modern focus may tell us more about the twentieth century than about the late Middle Ages. In our industrialized corner of the globe, where food supplies do not fail, we scarcely notice grain or milk, ever-present supports of life, and yearn rather after money or sexual favours as signs of power and of success.[43]

Notice the tone of Bynum's paragraph. It addresses topics of universal interest like sex, money, and food, but it does so calmly and methodically. You do not need to drop a bomb to get your reader's attention. Be relevant, but be gentle. People prefer to read essays that they find agreeable, trustworthy, and authoritative. Even when you suspect that your audience may disagree with you, it behooves you to treat them with some moderation. Put them in the right frame of mind to listen to your argument.

State Your Intellectual Interests Early

In the example above, Bynum caught the reader's attention by appealing to some personal interests. Your readers will also expect you to give them a sense of your intellectual interests. What are the broader historical problems that your essay addresses? Why have you chosen your specific topic to explore these interests? What argument will be developing over the course of your essay? Address these questions in the beginning of your essay, or else you will run the risk of confusing and losing your readers.

One introduction that answers these questions comes from an article by Michel F. Girard about the 1990 Oka crisis. He begins in this way:

Today, stories of environmental catastrophes or development projects opposed by local populations fill our newspapers and news broadcasts. According to the Decima polling firm, public concern for human and environmental health rose from the fifth rank in 1985 to the top of the public agenda in 1989, above other problems such as unemployment, government deficits, and the state of the economy. Following publication of the Brundtland Report in 1987, the main stakeholders, from environmentalists and scientists to governments and business groups, seem to have found a common ground to discuss the difficult issue of how to promote environmental protection in growth-oriented market economies. Most agree that sustainable development can be achieved with a broader understanding of the world we live in. This begs the question of historians' possible contribution to help reach that goal. Can the study of the interrelationships between humans and their natural surroundings from a historical perspective offer useful information to decision-makers and populations facing difficult environmental choices? The following case study details how environmentalists and Aboriginals used historical information on the natural environment to counter a development project in the municipality of Oka (Quebec) before the crisis of July 1990.[44]

In this introduction, Girard captures the reader's interest by reminding us of the recently growing public concern about the environment. Then he quickly shows how this concern and the concerns of business interests for the protection of a growing economy are now increasingly viewed as mutually attainable through wide-ranging discussion that includes all points of view. This should catch the attention of anyone who is interested in protecting the health of both the environment and the economy and labour market. Girard follows with a question about how historical knowledge might help in this discussion. Anyone who has ever wondered about the relevance of historical study to modern-day issues should be intrigued to read his case study.

Girard argues for the inclusion of historical perspectives in modern debates on development. He suggests that lack of understanding of historical conditions and decisions can lead to serious mistakes that cause environmental damage and, in the Oka case specifically, social upheavals. His goal is not to attack anyone, but to encourage understanding of the importance of historical knowledge by pointing out the harm that ignorance of the historical background can do. Girard starts to build his case very quickly by telling his audience why they should be interested, what are the problems he is addressing, and how he plans to approach them. This is a rich article, full of intriguing ideas, and Girard involves his reader immediately.

Build Your Essay with Good Paragraphs

A paragraph is much more than just an indented block of text. Good paragraphs develop inferences from sources, and they also contribute to the overall argument of the essay. To accomplish all this, the best paragraphs do the following things:

1. *Make a Transition from the Previous Paragraph.* Readers want to know the reasons why they are moving from one paragraph to the next. Good paragraphs connect to each other with one or two transition sentences, signposts that remind readers where they have been and that also tell them where they are going.

2. State the Argument of the Paragraph. Each paragraph presents and develops an argument that supports the overall development of the essay. Sometimes the argument may be located in the transition or "signpost" sentences; other times you may wish to write a separate "thesis sentence."

3. Present Evidence to Support the Argument of the Paragraph. What sort of evidence do you have to support the argument of this paragraph? Present the information from your sources that has helped you to make historical inferences.

In the abstract, these three components of the paragraph sound easy to manage. In fact, it takes discipline and creativity to practice this advice. The best historical writers write paragraphs that blend together a transition, an argument, and evidence, but there are many ways to do this. There is not one, common structure for every paragraph.

If you are looking for a model of successful paragraphing, consider Daniel Headrick's history of the global spread of European technologies, *The Tools of Empire*. In the fourth chapter, Headrick discusses how firearms changed during the nineteenth century:

> At the beginning of the nineteenth century the standard weapon of the European infantryman was the muzzle-loading smoothbore musket. It had a flintlock to detonate the powder through a hole in the breech and a bayonet that could be attached to the barrel for hand-to-hand combat. The Brown Bess, which British soldiers used until 1853, was much the same weapon their forefathers had carried at Blenheim in 1704. It had an official range of 200 yards but an effective one of 80, less than that of a good bow. Despite admonitions to withold their fire until they saw the whites of their enemies' eyes, soldiers commonly shot away their weight in lead for every man they killed. These muskets took at least a minute to load, so to maintain a steady rate of fire on the battlefield, soldiers were drilled in the coun-

termarch, each rank advancing in turn to shoot, then falling back to reload.

One of the most serious drawbacks of the flintlock muskets was their poor firing record. Under the best conditions, they fired only seven out of ten times, and in rain or damp weather they ceased firing altogether. For this reason soldiers were trained to use their weapons as pikes. In 1807, Alexander Forsyth, a Scottish clergyman and amateur chemist, offered a solution to this problem; using the violent explosive potassium chlorate as a detonating powder and a percussion lock instead of a flintlock, he made a gun that could fire in any weather. Tests showed that a percussion lock musket misfired only 4.5 times per thousand rounds, compared to 411 times for a flintlock. After 1814, Joshua Shaw of Philadelphia improved upon Forsyth's invention by putting the detonating powder into little metal caps, thereby simplifying the loading process and making the weapons even more impervious to the elements.[45]

Notice how Headrick makes the transition from the first to the second paragraph. In the first paragraph, he was discussing some of the drawbacks to the old muzzle-loading muskets. He begins the second paragraph by telling readers that he is now going to discuss one of the most *serious* problems. Readers are still learning from him about problems with muskets, but he is introducing them to a new way to evaluate the muskets. Headrick also presents plenty of evidence (and in the original text, each paragraph ends with a note to his sources). The paragraphs develop intellectually; they are supported by evidence; and they relate closely to the broader argument he is making about the history of firearms. Headrick's paragraphs guide readers by relating the significance of the evidence to his broader point.

Define Your Key Terms Early

Do not assume that you and your audience understand important concepts to mean the same thing. Define them as soon as you introduce them, preferably in the beginning of your essay. You will find that you can use a definition as a springboard to discuss the complexities of your subject.

1. Defining Uncommon Terms. Sometimes you will need to define specialized or foreign terms that your audience might not recognize. In his 1995 lecture to the History of Science Society on the subject of Arabic science, A.I. Sabra discussed the role of the *muwaqqit*. What, you may wonder, is a *muwaqqit*? According to Sabra, a *muwaqqit* is a timekeeper in a mosque who uses astronomical methods to determine the exact timing of the five daily prayers. But when Sabra defines this term, he takes the opportunity to discuss one of the things that makes Arabic science distinctive. According to him, "Through the introduction, apparently, for the first time under the Mamluks, of the office of *muwaqqit*, the timekeeper in charge of regulating the times of the five daily prayers, a place was created for the utilization of one form of scientific knowledge in a permanent religious institution." Sabra defines the word in such a way that it causes readers to think of a larger problem: the relations between religion and science.[46]

2. Redefining Common Terms. *Muwaqqit* demands definition, but sometimes you will even need to redefine commonly used English words like "landscape." This is exactly what William Cronon does in his book *Changes in the Land*. The *Canadian Oxford Dictionary* defines landscape as "natural or imaginary scenery as seen in a broad view," but Cronon uses the word more broadly. When he looks at the ecological transformation of colonial New England, he tells a story that relates the management of natural resources to cultural and political debates among the Native Americans and English settlers. Cronon's New Englanders saw that the "landscape was a visible confirmation of the state of human society."[47] An English landscape, a way of viewing and ordering the world, prevailed over a Native American landscape.

Set an Appropriate Tone

All historians must build a relationship with their audience. The best way to establish rapport is to find an appropriate, trustworthy tone.

1. Avoid the First Person Singular. Generally speaking, historical writers do not write in the first person singular. Historians all recognize that personal biases enter historical writing—there is usually no need to overemphasize it. A weak historical writer would state, "In my opinion, Margaret Ormsby ignored the role of the First Nations in the development of British Columbian society." The writer might just as well say, "Margaret Ormsby ignored the role of the First Nations in the development of British Columbian society," and spare readers the extra verbiage. Readers may confidently infer that this is the writer's opinion.

Usually historians employ the first person singular only when they have personally experienced a phenomenon they are describing. They introduce this personal information to explain their own relationship to the subject matter. For example, Carl Degler begins his book about racial thinking in anthropology, *In Search of Human Nature*, by writing, "Like most white Americans of my sex and class (the son of a fireman) and my generation (born in 1921) I came into a world that soon made me a racist and a sexist."[48] He does this to draw the reader's attention to personal and social issues of bias. He also honestly informs readers that he bears a close personal relationship to his subject, something they may wish to know when they evaluate his arguments.

2. Be Judicious and Dispassionate. All historians pass judgment on their subjects, but don't be too heavy-handed. If your subjects engaged in some particularly horrible activity, it is important to strike a balance between the rendering of judgment and the presentation of evidence. Some of the most difficult evidence to handle comes from Nazi Germany, and the following two historians built trustworthy arguments by using judicious, dispassionate tones.

Psychiatrist and historian Robert Jay Lifton wanted to learn why medical doctors served the Nazi regime. He uses Dr. Josef Mengele as a case in point, a distasteful case indeed. Lifton writes in his book *The Nazi Doctors* that Mengele "committed real crimes, murderous crimes, direct murder . . . These crimes included selections, lethal injections, shootings, beatings, and other forms of deliberate killing." All this is well-known, but the power of Lifton's work comes from his judicious argumentation. He describes Mengele's "research" in a matter-of-fact way, and puts Mengele's experiments in the context of the Nazi's medical career: "More than any other SS doctor, Mengele realized himself in Auschwitz. There he came into his own—found expression for his talents." Mengele remained the consummate clinical researcher, even in the midst of a concentration camp. Lifton presents Mengele objectively and ironically, so that readers will trust the book's conclusion: that Mengele had a schizoid personality, making it easier for him to detach himself from the suffering he inflicted on others.[49]

It is often enough just to describe a horrible activity in a subtle and ironic way. Your readers will understand that you have chosen to describe this activity because you find it repugnant. William Sheridan Allen wanted to learn how the Nazis came to power. Instead of focusing on well-known politicians in Berlin, he wrote a book called *The Nazi Seizure of Power* that focuses on the activities of the Nazi Party (NSDAP) in a small German town called Northeim. He describes how the Nazis used public events to sustain enthusiasm for their cause:

> Then on Sunday, March 19, the Northeim NSDAP gave its victory celebration, fittingly held in the Cattle Auction Hall. The hall, decorated with swastika flags, was full to the bursting point with at least a thousand people. The chief speaker was the Nazi preacher, Pastor Muenchmeyer, and his topic: "What a Transposition Through Divine Disposition!" The whole tone of the celebration was conservative, solemn, and religious.[50]

Allen does not call the Nazis cattle; the Cattle Auction Hall is an appropriate place for their meeting. He does not say that the pastor and his audience are intellectual mediocrities; he gives the title of the speech. Allen makes his point—that the Nazis were dangerous, obsequious drones—cleverly and subtly in a reasoned tone.

Treat Other Writers with Consideration

Scholarship is a very fragile enterprise. It thrives on lively debate and open disagreement, but it depends on mutual respect and careful consideration. When you write about other historians, give them the same amount of respect you would give if you were speaking to them in person. Do not oversimplify or misconstrue the arguments of your opponents, and do not make personal attacks on opponents in order to discredit their arguments.

Account for Counterarguments

Do not select one argument and ignore all the other possibilities. When you acknowledge the possibility of alternative interpretations you increase the credibility and complexity of your own work. Your readers will not think you are weak; they will think you are open-minded. In fact, your readers may already be aware of some possible contradictions to your argument, and they will expect you to deal with them.

By the very nature of their work, historians know it is impossible to write a flawless interpretation of anything. Knowledge is a slippery thing. In a short essay, it is often effective to note a few main counterarguments toward the end, and then conclude by re-asserting the reasons why you still wish to articulate your own position. In a longer essay, thesis, or book, authors often engage in multiple counterarguments as they consider the evidence.

One such example of counterargumentation can be found in Robert McElvaine's book, *Eve's Seed: Biology, the Sexes, and the Course of History*. McElvaine reviews evidence from prehistory and also from evolutionary psychology that suggests that humans are adaptable social animals who are both competitive and cooperative. Their cooperative side inclines them to build families and groups in which both sexes work together. For most of human history, differences between the sexes did not necessarily result in the subordination of one sex to another. McElvaine argues that it was the Agricultural Revolution, starting around 10,000 BCE, that caused men to subordinate women in almost every culture. According to McElvaine, men lost their roles as hunters, then, out of insecurity and envy, they turned to misogyny. Patriarchy in the home mirrored male domination in politics, religion, and business. Male domination is not natural; it can be explained historically.

To make this argument, McElvaine has to address two possible counterarguments: that human behaviour is completely determined by biology, and the opposite argument, that all people are born with a clean slate, and that it is nurture, not nature, that is important.

McElvaine wants to show that nature and nurture are both important. First, he engages these two opposite positions with a joke. Quoting his own father in an early chapter title, he writes that people are "90 percent nature and 90 percent nurture." Next he moves to consider the "nurture" position, espoused by many contemporary American liberals. McElvaine writes:

> The reason that so many liberals have clung to their insistence that human nature should be ignored is, I believe, a fundamental misapprehension concerning the implications of human nature. They have feared that the admission of the existence of innate characteristics will lead to findings on how people *differ*. In fact, the real meaning of human nature, as [Franz] Boas understood, is to be found in showing the ways in which people are *alike*. As Robert Wright has said, unlike the old social Darwinists, "today's Darwinian anthropologists, in scanning the world's peoples, focus less on surface differences among cultures than on deep unities."

After considering the "liberal" position, McElvaine turns to the "conservatives," who often believe in the determining power of genetics over human nature. He quotes from the work of Richard Dawkins and Edward Wilson, two "sociobiologists" who have written that people "are machines created by our genes," and that "Human behaviour . . . is the circuitous technique by which human genetic material has been and will be kept intact. Morality has no other demonstrable ultimate function." In response to these "biodeterministic" arguments, McElvaine writes:

> As Darwinism had been a century and more ago, sociobiology has been latched onto by people who seek to justify the unjustifiable. Conservatives seize on the principle of natural selection to maintain that everything that exists should be left alone, because it was made that way by the god of adaptation. But this is not so. It ignores genetic drift, whereby characteristics come into being that provide no evolutionary advantage, but also no disadvantage, and so survive despite Darwinian selection, not because of it. The actual essence of the Darwinian principle of selection is not that a trait must be well adapted in order to survive, but that it not be *poorly* adapted relative to other traits. It is possible for some features to continue to develop after they have fulfilled their original evolutionary function. Human intellectual ability is probably an example of this. It grew far beyond what was necessary for

human survival in the eons during which it was physically developing (although perhaps not beyond or even up to what is necessary for survival in the nuclear age; indeed it may yet prove to be ultimately maladaptive by destroying the species).

McElvaine's summary of the conservative and liberal positions on human nature is balanced and fair-minded, even though he strongly disagrees with these views. By reporting and engaging opposing arguments, McElvaine makes it more likely that liberals and conservatives will consider his argument, that liberal views on social and gender equality are actually supported by biological evidence about human nature.[51]

Lead Your Readers to an Interesting Conclusion

Over the course of your essay, you will develop the significance of your claims. All your analysis should sustain your main argument in interesting ways. As you lead your readers to their destination, give them plenty of signposts and evidence in the paragraphs. By the time you reach your concluding paragraph, your readers will be ready for you to put your ideas back into a broader context.

There is no formula for a concluding paragraph, just as there is no formula for an introductory or supporting paragraph. Even so, there are certain things that historians look for in a conclusion. A conclusion must reflect on the essay and answer the "Who cares?" question once again. A strong conclusion will not simply repeat the introduction. If the essay has truly developed and sustained an idea in an interesting way, then there should be a new way to sum things up. How are the findings of the essay significant? How might the findings of the essay change the way the readers think?

One example of a concise but interesting conclusion can be found in Veronica Strong-Boag's article "Home Dreams: Women and the Suburban Experience in Canada, 1945–60," which discusses the growth of residential suburbs after the Second World War and the impact that post-war housing initiatives had on Canadian women. While the new residential suburbs promised some attractive benefits for women, they also tended to isolate homemakers and, in a variety of ways, increased the demands made on women. She concludes:

Accounts from suburban women rarely match the image presented by Friedan and the critics of mass society. Their experiences were neither homogeneous nor uncomplicated. They were much more than merely the female counterparts of "organization men." Women were both victims and beneficiaries of a nation's experiment with residential enclaves that celebrated the gendered division of labour. Suburban dreams had captured the hopes of a generation shaken by war and depression, but a domestic landscape that presumed that lives could be reduced to a single ideal inevitably failed to meet the needs of all Canadians after 1945. In the 1960s the daughters of the suburbs, examining their parents' lives, would begin to ask for more.[52]

Strong-Boag summarizes her argument but she goes beyond it to suggest in the final sentence that there was a broader significance and a signpost to the future embedded in the development of suburban life.

⊰ 7 ⊱

NARRATIVE TECHNIQUES
FOR HISTORIANS

You may decide to organize your essay into one long narrative, or you may organize it along analytical lines, using short narratives to illustrate particular points of analysis. The narrative approach is often used in political and intellectual history, while analytical organization is often used in social, cultural, and economic history.

Write a Narrative to Tell a Story

Every narrative has some easily recognized components. A narrative has a narrator; it is organized chronologically; it develops a story; and it has main characters, a plot, and a setting. Historical narratives share many features with other forms of storytelling, such as novels and epic poems. During the fifth century BCE, a Greek adventurer and storyteller named Herodotus wrote one of the first historical narratives. He used dramatic tension and colorful description to help his readers imagine the past. While re-creating the Persian invasion of Greece in 480 BCE, Herodotus described how the emperor Xerxes and his huge army destroyed the small contingent of Spartans guarding the pass at Thermopylae. Herodotus did not simply say that the outnumbered Spartans were brave and fought to the death. Herodotus did not just tell readers that the Spartans were calm when the massive Persian forces came into sight; he told how the Spartans ignored the Persians and combed their hair. Instead of describing every episode of bravery, Herodotus selected the story of one Spartan soldier named Dieneces for special mention:

> It is said before the battle he was told by a native of Trachis that, when the Persians shot their arrows, there were so many of them that they hid the sun. Dieneces, however, quite unmoved by the thought of the strength of the Persian army, merely remarked: "This is pleasant news . . . if the Persians hide the sun, we shall have our battle in the shade."[53]

Write a Narrative to Support an Argument

Herodotus was not just telling a story about a gutsy warrior at Thermopylae. He was selecting specific events to illustrate a broader interpretation. Historians use such anecdotes and stories to make arguments, and the best storytellers can wrap a powerful argument within a seamless narrative. When Herodotus presented his work to the Athenian public, he used dramatic techniques to make a connection with his audience: Xerxes lost the war because he had too much pride, the downfall of many a character in Greek drama. Herodotus told the story of Thermopylae because he wanted to show in a colorful way that the Spartans had fought bravely in defense of a united Greece. He also wanted to draw a stark contrast between the Greeks who died willingly for their liberty and the Persians who had to whip their troops to make them fight.[54] The Greeks were clearly superior. Herodotus, like other historians, used a narrative to make an argument.

Combine Chronology with Causation

In narratives, historians use time to give structure to the past. For this reason, narratives have some obvious chronological features: a beginning, a middle, and an end. This may seem simple, but in the hands of a skilled historian a narrative's events do not just follow each other: early events cause subsequent events to happen.

If you are crafting a narrative, your first task will be to select influential events and then place them in chronological order. This is vital to understanding the causes of things, and it is not as easy as you may think. For example, historians draw on the accounts of both Muslims and Christians when they write about the Crusades. Unfortunately the two religions kept different calendars, meaning that historians must translate the dates of one into the dates of the other in order to form a coherent chronology. Sometimes you will not know a firm date for an event, meaning that you must do your best to place it in relation to another source. Eighteenth-century English parish records tell when children were baptized, not when they were born. If you wish to establish an individual's date of birth, you will have to find another source that tells you how long families and churches waited before baptizing their children. Placing events in a chronology is more than just an exercise: it helps you to understand change over time.

Get a Sense of Change and Continuity

When you have established the sequence of events, you will begin to get a sense of how some things changed over time while other things remained the same. Which events were entirely predictable in the context of the times? Which events were unexpected? This is not as easy as it sounds. Different historical actors might have interpreted the same continuities and changes differently. In 1833, the British Parliament emancipated all colonial slaves. Politicians and activists had been debating abolishing the slave trade, ameliorating the lives of slaves, and emancipating them from bondage for more than thirty years. From the perspective of London, some people may have seen emancipation as predictable and maybe even inevitable. From the perspective of a Barbadian slave who may not have been able to keep abreast of London politics, emancipation may have come as a sudden and dramatic change in status. But even that interpretation may be too simple. After emancipation, former masters invented numerous ways to coerce former slaves. Sugar production still required land, labour, and capital, all of which remained available to plantation owners and unavailable to former slaves. Former slaves may have felt more continuity than change.[55] In any case, it would be difficult to sort out such problems without establishing a firm chronology.

Select the Key Participants in Your Story

If you were telling a narrative of emancipation in Barbados, you might choose to focus on former slaves and masters. You might also work on slave women entrepreneurs, previously freed townsmen, colonial bankers, or government officials. Remember, your story must make an argument. Do certain individuals illustrate the argument of your narrative better than others? Were certain individuals more significant agents of change than others? You may wish to exclude some people from your narrative altogether, or you may wish to relegate them to the background.

Find Your Own Voice as a Narrator

Discovering your own voice as a narrator will be especially challenging the first time you try it. Every historian does this differently, but one rule always applies: every narrator must be as faithful as possible to the people and events of the past.

1. The Omniscient Narrator. Some historians prefer to recede into the background, telling their story from the perspective of an omniscient outsider while refraining from making comments about themselves or their engagement with the source materials. In his account of India's anticolonial rebellion of 1857, *The Great Mutiny*, Christopher Hibbert uses this style of narration. He is arguing that the rebellion began when British officers ordered Indian troops (*sepoys*) to use a new kind of bullet cartridge:

> One day in January 1857 a low-caste labourer at Dum-Dum asked a sepoy for a drink of water from his *lota*. The sepoy, being a Brahmin, had naturally refused: his caste would not allow him to grant such a request; he had just scoured his *lota*; the man would defile it by his touch. "You will soon lose your caste altogether," the labourer told him. "For the Europeans are going to make you bite cartridges soaked in cow and pork fat. And then where will your caste be?"[56]

2. The Uncertain Narrator. Not all historians feel that their sources permit such an omniscient narration. In fact, great controversy surrounds the origins of the 1857 rebellion. Sometimes historians use less certain strategies of narration to reveal the ambiguities of their source materials. Writers can strengthen a narrative by informing readers of the limits of their interpretations. John Demos uses such a strategy in a book called *The Unredeemed Captive*, which is about Eunice Williams, an English girl who was captured by Mohawks in the Deerfield Massacre of 1704. After her abduction, Eunice adapted to the ways of the Kahnawake Iroquois. This disturbed her family but it did not stop them from trying to bring her back to Massachusetts. Demos worked with limited sources, mostly the letters and diaries of Eunice's English relatives. The family spent decades trying to learn about Eunice, but in the end they recorded very little information. Demos struggled to extract meaning from these scarce sources, but his narrative is at its most compelling when he speculates about the changes in Eunice's life:

> Different it was, very different. And yet, within a relatively short time, it took. By 1707, Eunice was reported to be "unwilling to return." And the Indians—including, one would presume, her new family—"would as soon part with their hearts" as with this successfully "planted" child.[57]

Choose Your Own Beginning and End

The past is interconnected across chronological and geographical boundaries, but every narrative must have a beginning and an end. You will find it challenging to decide when to start and stop your story. Hibbert begins his story of the 1857 rebellion with a description of a typical working day for Sir Thomas Metcalfe, British representative to the king of Delhi.

> He returned from his office at half past two for dinner at three. After dinner he sat reading for a time before going down to the billiard-room. A game of billiards was followed by two hours spent on the terrace contemplating the river. Then it was time for a light supper and an evening hookah. Immediately the clock struck eight, he stood up and went to bed, un-

doing his neckcloth and throwing it, together with his well-tailored coat, on to the floor to be picked up by the appropriate servant. If this or any other servant did not perform his duties to the master's entire satisfaction, Sir Thomas would send for a pair of white kid gloves which were presented to him on a silver salver. These he would draw on with becoming dignity, then firmly pinch the culprit's ear.[58]

Hibbert is not just telling a story about an indolent, autocratic colonial official. Hibbert uses the beginning to set the scene for a larger story about how Indians rebelled against British authority, how British forces crushed the rebels after great loss of life, and how this experience transformed South Asia and the British Empire. Hibbert sets the opening scene in Delhi because his narrative will reach its climax when the British recapture the city. His narrative ends when the British banish the king of Delhi:

The trial lasted more than two months; but the verdict was never in doubt. On 29 March he was found guilty on all charges and later sentenced to be transported for life to Rangoon. He left Delhi in October accompanied by Jawan Bakht, another young son whom he had had by a concubine, and by a most unwilling Zinat Mahal who, by now "quite tired of him," described him as " troublesome, nasty, cross old fellow." He died on 7 November 1862 in Rangoon where the descendants of his son, Jawan Bakht, are still living today.[59]

Hibbert concludes his narrative at this point for a number of reasons. The rebellion ended in many different ways for many different people, but for Hibbert, the exile of the king of Delhi represents the end of the rebellion. One of the causes of the rebellion had been a dispute over who would succeed the king of Delhi. Much of the rebellion had taken place in and around Delhi. The exile of the king draws several strands of the story to a close, while Hibbert mentions the descendants of the king as a way of emphasizing the enduring legacy of the rebellion. Follow Hibbert's example when you conclude a historical narrative: choose a beginning and an ending that suits your story and your argument.

⪥ 8 ⪤

WRITING SENTENCES IN HISTORY

Historians share a common goal with all writers: to communicate ideas effectively. Historians differ from other writers on some of the conventions for achieving this goal. This causes some confusion among writers who hail from other disciplines, but even so, no historical convention is arbitrary; all of them help historians to represent the past as accurately as possible. While you are writing and revising, use these conventions to your advantage.

Choose Verbs That Are Precise

Verbs form the heart of every sentence because they convey the action. Every writer should select precise verbs and avoid vague ones, and this principle is decidedly true for historians.

What is a vague verb? For starters, verbs of being are vague, but as you can see, sometimes it is difficult to avoid them. The order of ideas in the sentence may dictate that you use "is," "are," or another form of the verb "to be." Still, beginning writers tend to overuse verbs of being, a problem that drains the color out of their writing. Why write "Queen Victoria was regnant for sixty-four years" when you can write "Queen Victoria reigned for sixty-four years"? If you find yourself writing with a verb of being, look for a noun or an adjective that has a precise verb counterpart.

Make Passive Sentences Active

Historians try to avoid the passive voice. One of the purposes of historical writing is to uncover who did what, when. The worst thing a historian can do is to create silence and confusion about the past, which is what the passive voice often does. The passive voice can obliterate historical actors altogether: "New France was surrendered in September 1760." By whom? If you cannot write an active sentence like "Governor Vaudreuil surrendered New France to General Amherst in September 1760" with any certainty, then you owe your readers an explanation.

As you read more history, you will start to notice that passive sentences often indicate weak reasoning. This is true of history, but it is not necessarily true of other disciplines. Some authors, especially natural scientists, use the passive voice to downplay their personal involvement in research. In fact, one of the biggest challenges for historians of science is to cut through this prose and learn just how scientists did involve themselves in research.

There are circumstances when it is appropriate for historians to use the passive voice, and the best writers might include one or two passive sentences on a page. You may wish to put a historical subject at the end of a sentence: "New France was surrendered by Governor Vaudreuil," which may be the best place for Vaudreuil, depending on the order of ideas in the sentence or the paragraph. But even though there are some circumstances when passive verbs are appropriate, passive sentences often confuse the order of ideas. They should be used sparingly. (In that passive sentence, it was important to emphasize the word "sparingly.")

Write in the Past Tense

Unlike writers in other disciplines, historians write almost everything in the past tense. This is not an arbitrary peculiarity. Writing in the past tense helps historians to place people and events in an intelligible chronological order.

Historians prefer the past tense, but verb tense is often the subject of some confusion. This is largely because scholars who write about literature have a different set of conventions. A literary critic might write "In *Black Boy*, Richard Wright speaks eloquently and forcefully against American racism and capitalism." Wright's words ring just as true today as they did in 1937 when he wrote them. For the purposes of writing about literature, the present tense gives an author's ideas a sense of immediacy.

Literary classics have a powerful effect on readers today, but historians want to place Wright's novel within the context of his life and times. Wright does not really speak today—he died in 1960. He wrote *Black Boy* during the Great Depression, when he joined the growing American communist party. At the time readers interpreted Wright's work differently than they do today. Using the present tense confuses the chronology of Wright's life and times, while using the past tense enables writers to arrange one event in relationship to another. Historians usually write in the present tense only when they are discussing recent works or living scholars.

Avoid Split Infinitives If You Can

In English, the infinitive is formed by adding the preposition "to," as in "to be or not to be." Shakespeare could have split the infinitive and written "to bravely be or not to be," but that would have prompted the audience to throw vegetables. Generally speaking, it is a bad idea to place words between "to" and the verb. It throws off the logical order of ideas in the sentence.

Even so, there are circumstances when it is appropriate to split an infinitive. Sometimes it just sounds better. There is a good reason why Star Trek begins with the phrase "to boldly go where no man has gone before." If the infinitive is put back together, listen to the result: "To go boldly where no man has gone before." How uninspiring. In this case, a split infinitive is better than having an adverb in an unnatural location.

Put Verbs in Your Sentences

Theoretically, a sentence can be a sentence only if it has a verb. And yet, as you can see from the "How uninspiring" sentence above, it is possible to use a verbless sentence as an interjection, and there are other uses for them, too. Verbless sentences do add punch and colour to writing, but they really do not have a place in formal writing, which is the kind of writing that historians usually do. When you write a verbless sentence in a work of history, you are inviting your reader to apply the red ink.

Put Your Ideas in an Intelligible Order

You must put your ideas in an order that your audience will understand. This is not as easy as it sounds. After weeks of reading and research on a historical topic, you will be steeped in the complexities of how people, ideas, and events are interrelated. But when you write, you must unravel that complexity and place your ideas in a sequence of words. In each sentence, you must imagine what your audience needs to know first, second, and third.

Keep Related Words Together

You may think it makes sense to say "The tail-gunner saw a cloud form over Hiroshima in the shape of a mushroom," because you already know how these ideas are related. Nevertheless, your audience can only get a sense of the relationship of ideas from the way you place the words, and in this case the words are placed poorly. After all, the shape of the mushroom does not relate to Hiroshima, it relates to the cloud. The audience would understand the sentence better if you wrote, "The tail-gunner saw a mushroom-shaped cloud form over Hiroshima." If you keep related words together, you will lead readers seamlessly through your sentence. If you keep unrelated words together, readers will have to pause and sort out the jumble.

Keep Pronouns Close to the Words They Represent

By definition, a pronoun substitutes for a noun, but your readers must know which noun. You know in your head which pronoun relates to which noun, but your readers must infer the relationship from the way you place the words, and you must leave them in no doubt.

The best way to avoid misunderstanding is to place the pronoun close to the noun it modifies. Here is a sentence with a confusing pronoun: "John A. Macdonald's 1864 partnership with George Brown demonstrated his political practicality and flexibility." Does "his" refer to Macdonald or to Brown? "His" is closer to "Brown," and your reader may infer that "his" represents Brown. This may not, however, be your meaning. Anyone who knows about the Canadas of the 1860s knows that both Brown and Macdonald were talented politicians, both of whom could be described as pratical and flexible. Macdonald is often described even as "wily," so is it safe to assumne that "his" refers to Brown? Your sentence is unclear.

Keep Subjects and Verbs Close Together

The principal relationship in a sentence is between the subject and the verb. Do not put too much between them. Take a look at this sentence: "Grey Owl, after two years with the Canadian army in the First World War, spent his life as a hunter, guide, and conservationist." In order to read this sentence, you must hold "Grey Owl" in the back of your mind until you find out what he is doing. The sentence would express the ideas more effectively if it were rewritten like this: "After two years with the Canadian army in the First World War, Grey Owl spent his life as a hunter, guide, and conservationist." Generally speaking, it is acceptable to place a short statement in between a subject and verb, as in "Grey Owl, originally called Archie Belaney, spent his life as a hunter, guide, and conservationist." Just don't put too much between a subject and its verb.

Begin a Sentence on Common Ground and Gradually Build a New Point

Writing a sentence is not just about arranging the ideas in an orderly way. In history, as in all writing, a sentence is a place to develop an idea. A well-written sentence gives the reader a sense of direction.

Start by summarizing the previous sentence or by mentioning an idea that you and your reader hold in common; then build toward your original point. A weak pair of sentences would say "General Lee's horse was named Traveller. Fine horses were hard to find in those years, but Traveller was one of the best." The reader has to jump from Traveller to a general statement about horses and then back to Traveller. A better pair of sentences would build from Traveller toward a general statement about horses: "General Lee's horse was named Traveller. He was one of the best horses at a time when good horses were hard to find." The first sentence moves from General Lee to Traveller; then the second sentence moves from Traveller to a general statement about horses. The sentences have a smooth connection.

The Emphasis Comes at the End

If you are developing your ideas over the course of a sentence, then the end of the sentence should be interesting and emphatic. One master of emphatic writing (and speaking) was Winston Churchill. Here is what Churchill wrote about the Crusades in one of his books, *The Birth of Britain*:

> The Crusading spirit had for some time stirred the minds of men all over western Europe. The Christian kingdoms of Spain had led the way with their holy wars against the Arabs. Now, towards the end of the eleventh century, a new enemy of Christendom appeared fifteen hundred miles to the east. The Seljuk Turks were pressing hard upon the Byzantine Empire in Asia Minor, and harassing devout pilgrims from Europe through Syria to the Holy Land.[60]

Notice how each sentence begins with a connection to the previous sentence. Also notice how each sentence develops in a new direction and concludes with a new idea. The second sentence is especially skillful. It begins by saying something specific about the western European Christians, but then leads readers to consider the enemies of the Christians, the Arabs.

Construct Parallel Forms for Emphasis

One of the best tricks for writing an effective sentence is to learn how to use a parallel construction. This is a kind of repetition in which related ideas are expressed in a rigorously similar grammatical form. For example, on October 8, 1940, as Nazi bombers were pounding Britain, Churchill told the House of Commons that "Death and sorrow will be the companions of our journey; hardship our garment; constancy and valour our only shield. We must be united, we must be undaunted, we must be inflexible."[61] He constructed the first sentence loosely around the repetition of "our," but he constructed the second sentence tightly around the repetition of "we must be." In a parallel construction, a writer expresses parallel ideas by using a parallel grammatical structure.

Form the Possessive Correctly

Thus far, this book has not delved into grammar because this has been the subject of many other guides to writing. Chances are that if you are now learning how to write history, you have already learned how to write a grammatical sentence. Even so, it is embarrassing to note that many historians, including some well-known professionals, often make one particular grammatical error: they do not know how to form the possessive. Most of the confusion surrounds words that end in the letter *s*.

1. *Form the Possessive of a Singular Noun by Adding 's.* This is true even when the word ends in the letter *s*. For example, it is correct to write "Cecil Rhodes's diamond mines," or "the duchess's letters."

There are some minor exceptions to this rule. Traditionally, ancient names ending in *s* take only an apostrophe, as in "Moses' laws" or "Jesus' name." However, these constructions are sufficiently awkward that many writers form the possessive with *of*, as in "the laws of Moses" or "the name of Jesus."

2. *Form the Possessive of a Plural Noun by Adding an Apostrophe.* This is true when the plural is formed by adding an *s*, for example, "the Redcoats' muskets" or "the Wright brothers' airplane."

3. *Don't Bother Using an Apostrophe to Form the Plural of Abbreviations and Numbers.* It used to be standard practice to use apostrophes to form plurals, for example, "PC's were first manufactured during the 1980's." Most style manuals now consider this use of the apostrophe to be old-fashioned. Omit the apostrophe and just write "PCs" and "the 1980s." Use an apostrophe to form a plural only when there is the possibility of confusion, as in "There are two o's and two p's in apostrophe."

4. Don't Use an Apostrophe to Form the Plural. It is incorrect to write that "Columbus discovered the America's." Columbus discovered the Americas, at least according to some people.

Break the Rules If You Must

You will find that on occasion the conventions listed above will lead you to perform some unnecessary gymnastics. These conventions may even cause you to write an ugly, unnatural sentence. In all such cases, break the rules. Good historical writers understand the spirit of the law as well as the letter. Your first task is to get your meaning across, and to do it persuasively.

✠ 9 ✠

CHOOSE PRECISE WORDS

Word choice can make all the difference to a historian, so choose your words precisely. The past abounds with catastrophic examples of poorly chosen words. One such example is the 1840 Treaty of Waitangi, in which the British took New Zealand from the Maoris by mistranslating the word for "sovereignty."[62] This deliberate act of imprecision has caused a century and a half of bad feelings. Chances are that you will never be deliberately imprecise, but you should still choose your words very carefully. Get in the habit of checking your essays for word choice, which is also known as diction. The basic rules of diction often strike inexperienced writers as arbitrary. They are not. The more we read, the more we see that some words are commonly used together, and some are not. Common diction ensures common understanding.

Be Concise

Some historical writers believe that they can demonstrate the complexity of their thoughts by writing sentences that are bursting with unnecessary words. They are wrong. If you make every word count, then you will give your readers the clearest possible picture of your ideas. Why write "It is an undeniable fact that William the Conqueror was instrumental in establishing the Norman regime" when you might easily say "William the Conqueror established the Norman regime"? If you can say something in seven words, why say it in sixteen? Being concise does not mean that all your sentences should be short and choppy; it means that you should not try your readers' patience.

Write in Language That Your Audience Can Understand

Most historians write in language that intelligent readers can understand. This standard is subjective, yet it does set history apart from many fields of writing that have developed specialized jargon. Sometimes outside jargon can creep into historical writing. For example, the dictionary defines "hegemony" as dominance, but for professional historians the word is associated with the theoretical writings of an Italian socialist named Antonio Gramsci. You may indeed be writing for an audience that understands hegemony in this precise way, but to a wider audience hegemony may be a jargon word that can cause a misunderstanding.

1. Literary Jargon.   History is a form of literature, and historians have learned a great deal from literary critics. Most people who study literature love the English language, but some, in their exuberance, have produced some dreadful writing. People who seem to be different have become the "subjectivized Other." People who like to read good history "valorize the narrativization of the Subject." It may be fun to commit random acts of capitalization, and it is often convenient to stick an "-ize" on a noun in order to create a verb, but if you are writing for more than just a few literary critics, write in a language that your audience can understand.

2. Social-science Jargon.   History is also one of the social sciences, and history is, in many ways, difficult to distinguish from the disciplines of anthropology, economics, political science, and sociology. Some social scientists write well, but many prefer tortured jargon to ordinary words. Talking is "interpersonal communication," and a different way of looking at something puts it on "another axis of differentiation." This language is fine for communicating with other social scientists, but really, when is the last time you freely chose to read a book by people who write like this? Social-science jargon will limit the size of your audience.

3. Legal Jargon.   Many historians study the law, and some historians even practice the law. Nevertheless, there are important differences between legal writing and historical writing. When lawyers compose legal documents, they are writing for a different audience: the court. They go to great lengths to ensure that their clients will not get into trouble. To avoid trouble, lawyers use archaisms, repetition, and formal words like "the said," "party to the first part," and "stipulate." This language is not pretty, and it should be used only by lawyers, for lawyers, unless stipulated to by both the party of the first part, who is hereby named the historian, and the party of the second part, which is hereby named the historian's audience. Otherwise, keep legal jargon out of historical writing.

4. Government Jargon.   "Officialese," as it is called, is a close cousin of legal jargon. They both have the same purpose: to cover the writer's hindquarters. At least lawyers have the excuse of having to protect their clients; bureaucrats, officers, and politicians use jargon mainly to protect themselves. Either they want to make themselves seem important or they are trying to avoid precise commitments. In his famous essay "Politics and the English Language," George Orwell translated the following passage from the Bible into the obscure, pompous language of government:

> I returned and saw under the sun, that the race is not to the swift, nor the battle to the strong, neither yet bread to the wise, nor yet riches to men of understanding, nor yet favour to men of skill; but time and chance happeneth to them all.

Here is Orwell's translation:

> Objective consideration of contemporary phenomena compels the conclusion that success or failure in competitive activities exhibits no tendency to be commensurate with innate capacity, but that a considerable element of the unpredictable must invariably be taken into account.[63]

Orwell's point is clear: jargon-writers are in the habit of taking concrete examples and beautiful rhythm and turning them into abstract language and meaningless words. Always use precise language that your audience understands.

Avoid Pretentious Language

Don't think that you will look smart just by using complicated words. You may only wind up confusing your readers. You may think that central planning had a "procrustean" effect on Soviet engineering, but if your audience does not know that the word means a ruthless disregard for special circumstances, you have not gained much ground with them. Even if they do know what the word means, it may stand out from the overall tone of your argument. Control any urges to use puffed-up vocabulary.

Avoid Colloquial Language

Most history instructors expect that you will write in formal English. This means that you should avoid slang, contractions, and an overly casual tone. Such informal language, also known as colloquial language, may be inserted as part of a quotation, and you may also use colloquial language outside of formal, academic writing. This book, for example, has a less formal tone than most works of history. Even so, most historians consider colloquial language to be, like, uncool.

Be Sensitive to the Politics of Diction

Historical writing has always reflected the politics of the times. Today historians are demonstrating their awareness of discrimination by avoiding intolerant language. Conservatives complain that liberals are forcing a "politically correct" form of "linguistic engineering" on them. Some liberals think that conservatives have not gone far enough to purge the language of offensive usage. The debate will never be resolved, but everyone can agree that writers must meet their audience. Historical writers must keep their eyes and ears open to learn what their audience thinks is appropriate. Some racial designations have changed considerably over the years: "Negro" and "coloured" changed to "black" and then "black" started to become "African-American." In Canada, other than in some legal connections, it is common to use the term "First Nations" rather than the outdated "Indians." If you are writing about one particular nation or band, you should use its specific name. Be aware, however, that modern groups and classifications do not necessarily coincide with social and political organization in the past. Also note that what is considered correct in terms of titles and spellings is constantly under debate: try to be informed about and sensitive to these debates. Most historians recognize that all traditions are invented, including linguistic traditions, and they also recognize that people ought to be allowed to come up with a name for themselves.

Be Sensitive to Gender-Specific Language

Oscar Wilde said, "Anybody can make history. Only a great man can write it." He said this in the 1890s, and his main point was to call attention to the difference between historical actors and the people who write about them. When historians read this statement today, Wilde's underlying sexist assumptions are readily apparent, even if Wilde might be forgiven for being a creature of his times.

In recent years historians have become more sensitive to gender. This is reflected not only in their intellectual interests but also in their historical writing. Years ago it was acceptable to say, "The historian must analyze sources. He must understand the relevant documents." The masculine pronoun with an antecedent of indeterminate gender was conventional. Fortunately, today there are plenty of female historians, a fact that contradicts the practice of associating nouns like "the historian" with masculine pronouns. Such a construction now seems inaccurate and biased.

To avoid such sexist pitfalls, you may be tempted to change the second sentence with some keyboard gymnastics: "He/she must understand the relevant documents," or, even worse, you might write "s/he." Add an "http://" and you will have created a new Internet address. Slashed pronouns can usually be prevented by employing simple solutions. First, consider using neutral pronouns like "everyone," "anybody," and "everybody." If that doesn't work, try to change the sentences from singular to plural. Just say, "Historians must analyze sources. They must understand the relevant documents." Changing a gender-specific singular to a gender-neutral plural conveys the same idea without any sexist overtones.

You might also be tempted to substitute the third-person-singular neutral pronoun, "one," for a gender-biased "he." "When one is a historian, one must analyze sources." Occasionally such a construction is appropriate, but most of the time it sounds pretentious.

Avoid Euphemisms

Sometimes "politically correct" language works well, but other times it seems silly. Some linguistic engineering may be necessary to overcome odious rhetorical practices, but nobody is really calling stupid people "intellectually challenged." This is a euphemism, a polite, meaningless word that covers up for a harsh reality. The twentieth century seems to have been especially rich in euphemisms: torched villages were "pacified," totalitarian regimes were "people's republics," and used cars were "pre-owned vehicles." Spare your readers the bull.

Choose Figurative Language Carefully

When historians write about subjects that are unfamiliar to their readers, it often helps to make an imaginative comparison with something the reader knows. These comparisons often take the form of metaphors and similes. It would be perfectly acceptable to write that "Simón Bolívar participated in the overthrow of Spanish rule in the Americas." It would be more engaging to write, "Simón Bolívar played a role in the overthrow of Spanish rule in the Americas," because this would draw a comparison to the theater. It would be even more colourful to say that "Simón Bolívar was the George Washington of Spanish America," but you might have to sustain the metaphor by comparing evidence about the two leaders. Metaphors and similes add colour to historical writing, but it takes practice to use them well.

Use Metaphors and Similes Judiciously

There are a number of ways for a metaphor to go awry. You could write that "Simón Bolívar was the John Chilembwe of Spanish America," but this metaphor presents a number of problems. Chances are that people reading an essay on Venezuelan history have never heard of John Chilembwe. This is unfortunate, because in 1913 Chilembwe led a major rebellion against British colonial rule in Nyasaland. Still, the metaphor does not work in a number of other ways. Chilembwe's rebellion failed while Bolívar's succeeded. The comparison is also awkward because it is anachronistic: Chilembwe's revolt happened a century after Bolívar's. It is a good idea to use vivid metaphors and similes, but they must ring true to your audience's ears.

Use Colour, but Avoid Clichés

Your readers will welcome colourful language, but they will find your colours boring if they are entirely predictable. Colourful expressions that have been overused are called clichés. Replace them with plain language or less predictable metaphors.

Use this simple test to spot a cliché. You are using a cliché if you can remove the last word from the phrase and your readers can automatically fill it in:

- "Queen Elizabeth did not suffer fools . . . (gladly)."
- "Albert Einstein burned the midnight . . . (oil)."
- "The bubonic plague reared its ugly . . . (head)."

Use Foreign Words That Are Familiar to Your Audience

Historians often use foreign words in their writing. Some foreign terms have come into common English usage, as in "Nehru was a politician *par excellence*," or "The US Constitution prohibits the *ex post facto* application of laws." However, when you write about the history of a foreign country you may sometimes find yourself in a quandary over how to use foreign terms.

The basic rule of thumb is to use terms that your audience understands. Imagine that you are writing about the history of the amaXhosa, an important group of people who live in South Africa. If you were taking a seminar on southern African history, and you were writing for an instructor who was a specialist in the field, it might be appropriate for you to spell out the name "amaXhosa." This is because specialists in southern African history know that this group of people forms the plural of their collective name by adding the prefix "ama." If you were writing for a more general audience, say, in a survey of world history, you would probably not want to bother teaching your readers about the intricacies of southern African prefixes. In this situation, it is probably best to call your subjects "the Xhosa," a compromise that shows your reader that you are savvy enough not to add English plurals to foreign words. It is important to know your audience and to meet them on common ground.

Check for These Common Diction Problems

It is easy to misuse words and expressions, partly because they are so often misused. Word-processing programs make it possible to search for any given word. If you suspect that you have misused any of the words listed below, run a search on your computer.

If you need further assistance on points of usage, ask a reference librarian to help you find *The New Fowler's Modern English Usage*, ed. R.W. Burchfield (Oxford: Oxford University Press, 1996). It is the updated version of H.W. Fowler's classic work on English usage, and it is the basis for the following list of common problems that appear in historical writing.

AD and BC mean *Anno domini* [the year of our Lord] and Before Christ, respectively. These abbreviations seem to be slipping out of use, in favor of the ecumenical euphemisms CE and BCE, which mean Common Era and Before Common Era. When you think about it, though, these abbreviations are not really much of an improvement.

All right is proper for formal writing. Many people spell it as "alright," but most authorities regard "alright" as overly casual. It may have been all right for Elvis to sing "That's alright, Mama," but it's not all right for you to write "alright" in a formal essay.

And/or appears frequently in insecure writing, possibly because it has a legalistic sound to it. "And/or" is not incorrect, but it is inelegant. It implies that the two items that are joined together can be taken apart, which is a fundamentally odd concept. As Burchfield says, it is usually a good idea to avoid it by writing "X or Y or both," or just by writing "or."

Ante- and **anti-** are two Latin prefixes that students often confuse. "Ante" means before, while "anti" means against. For example, "antebellum America" refers to America before the Civil War, whereas "antiwar protestors" opposed the war.

Because is a word commonly used in historical writing because historians usually want to learn what caused things to happen. "Letitia Youmans founded the first Canadian local of the Women's Christian Temperance Union because she was distressed by the effects of alcohol on family life." Elementary-school English teachers tell students not to start a sentence with "because," and generally speaking they are right. "Because" introduces a clause that depends on another clause; if you reverse the sentence about Letitia Youmans and start it with the "because" clause you will make it hard for readers to follow the sentence. You need to know what is being caused before you learn why it is being caused. Still, there are circumstances when historical writers make reasonable exceptions to this rule.

Cannot is usually written as one word, not as "can not." Furthermore, "can't" is usually too colloquial for academic writing.

Different is the subject of some debate. Real sticklers will tell you that "different" can only be followed by "from" and not by "than" or "to." The editors of the Oxford English Dictionary disagree. They say that people have been using "different to" since 1526 and "different than" since 1644. Is it possible that so many people could be so wrong for so long? Perhaps. Somehow, "different from" still sounds better.

Double negatives are not uncommon in historical writing, but they should be used sparingly. Two negatives always cancel each other out: "Napoleon was not undefeated at Waterloo" is a stupid way to say "Napoleon was defeated at Waterloo." Most of the time you would do well to convert a double negative into a positive. Sometimes double negatives can be used to add irony, as in the first sentence above.

Due to is a bullet worth dodging. You may think that this compound preposition is harmless enough, but generations of history professors have told students not to overuse it. According to Strunk and White, "due to" should be used only to mean "attributable to," as in "Custer's defeat was due to poor intelligence." It should not substitute for "because" or "through," as in "Custer lost the battle due to poor intelligence." Even so, both the proper and improper uses of "due to" are pretty vague. How can Custer's defeat be attributed to poor intelligence? It is impossible to know, even from the proper use of "due to." It might be best to avoid "due to" altogether.

It's and **its** get confused frequently, even though they mean two completely different things. "It's" is the contraction of "it is": "It's not too late to learn how to write history." "Its" is the possessive form of "it": "When Castro lit a Montecristo, its pungent smoke filled the air." If you confuse "it's" and "its," the only way to salvage your reputation is to tell your reader that it's a typo. It is also worth mentioning that "its'" is not a word in the English language.

Led to. It may be true that "the First World War *led to* the Second World War"; just don't confuse chronology with causation. It is true that 1939 follows 1914, but your readers will expect you to explain how the first war helped to cause the second war. Saying "led to" is often vague.

Lifestyle is an imprecise word that has no place in historical writing. This sentence comes from a student historian's essay: "The lifestyle of the African-American slaves cannot be compared with the lifestyle of the concentration camp inmates." The writer would have done better to discuss their ways of life, their cultures, or their experiences.

Native is a dangerous word to bandy about in historical writing. One might plausibly talk about the native Tahitians just as one might talk about the native French. But don't call the Tahitians "the natives" because you wouldn't call the French "the natives," except perhaps in jest. "The natives" is a term that Europeans once reserved for people from other parts of the world whom they deemed to be uncivilized. Today it is bad form to use this kind of derogatory language. Of course, every rule has its exceptions: the American Indians who live in the United States now prefer to be called the Native Americans. In Canada the most common term is the First Nations

Regard is misused frequently in compound prepositions like "with regards to" and "in regards to." The prime offenders are bureaucrats, but historical writers misuse "regard," too. There are two proper ways to use "regard." If it is part of a compound preposition, use the singular "regard," as in "with regard to" or "in regard to." If it is a verb, conjugate accordingly: "as it regards" or "as they regard."

That and **which** have become the subject of considerable confusion among historians and other writers. In the following sentences, which one would you use to connect one clause to another?

1. "Despite the tense atmosphere *that/which* prevailed during the trial, Mandela spoke his mind to the court."
2. "In 1846, the Corn Laws, *that/which* had protected English farmers from foreign competition, were repealed."

Fowler and Burchfield have tried to standardize the use of "that" and "which." They recommend that authors use "that" in restrictive clauses and "which" in nonrestrictive clauses. What do these grammatical terms mean?

The first example sentence is a restrictive clause. In other words, the information "prevailed during the trial" is essential to the statement "Despite the tense atmosphere." According to Fowler and Burchfield, the first sentence, and all restrictive clauses, should employ "that."

The second sentence is different because it contains a nonrestrictive clause: "had protected English farmers from foreign competition." This is a parenthetical statement that might just as well be placed in another sentence. If you want to use it in this sentence, use "which." Fowler and Burchfield recommend using "which" in all other nonrestrictive clauses, too.

If you apply Fowler and Burchfield's rule to your writing, you will attain a higher degree of clarity. Their rule does work well. Unfortunately, even Fowler and Burchfield admit that they are fighting an uphill battle for the proper use of "that" and "which." When you read other historical writers, apply the rule for "that" and "which" and you will notice that few know the difference.

Tribe is subject to the same rules that govern "native." A long time ago anthropologists defined tribe precisely, to mean a group of people who trace their ancestry to one person, real or imagined. Unfortunately, many historians and journalists use "tribe" loosely and offensively, to mean any group of people with brown skin. One might talk about "tribal conflict" in Rwanda but not "tribal conflict" in Bosnia. This use of the word "tribe" derives from efforts of European administrators to classify and regulate groups of people in their former colonies. Ironically, some Africans and Native Americans took up the practice and now call themselves "tribes."

Note for Canadian Students

Many historians in Canada prefer to use English spelling rather than American spelling, colour, for example, rather than color, centre rather than center. Others do not care very much, and will be happy to accept papers written in either spelling style. It is best to choose one style or the other, rather than mixing them, and the easiest way to accomplish this is to choose one dictionary and spell all such words in accordance with this specific dictionary. If in doubt on which spelling style to use, ask your instructor for guidance.

✢ 10 ✢

REVISING AND EDITING

This guide is not a cookbook for historians. There is no recipe for writing history, and if you follow the conventions set out in this book, there is no guarantee that your writing will become perfect. There is no such thing as a perfect history, and there is no such thing as a "cookbook historian."

Historians understand the conventions for writing history, but all historians have their own ways of writing. Approaches to writing depend partly on personal style and partly on the subject that is being written about. The more you write history, the more you will gain a sense of your own style and interests. And while you are learning about these things, you will also come to know your own strengths and weaknesses. You have probably heard of the ancient Greek inscription over the temple at Delphi: "Know thyself." Get to know your own weaknesses as a writer; then watch out for them.

Get Some Perspective on Your Draft

It is important to get some distance from your paper. You must write for an audience, and to do that you must be able to see your writing as someone else sees it. Spend a few days working on other things: putting some distance between yourself and your writing will help you to make revisions.

When historians are in the thick of writing, they often have to take a break before they can stand back and assess their own text with any objectivity. If you are lucky, you might have an instructor or friend who is willing to read a first draft and comment on it. In any case, write the best possible draft, and take your critic's comments seriously. Eventually, you will have to share your writing with an audience that is unfamiliar with all your sources and their unique problems. Early comments on a draft can help you assess whether you have made a persuasive case to your audience.

Revise Your Draft

A critical reader will assess both the strengths and weaknesses of your paper. Sometimes it is difficult to take criticism, but remember that your best critics spend a great deal of time thinking about your work. This in itself is a compliment. Even if you conclude that the critic's advice is bad, the criticism has had the positive effect of making you reconfirm your position.

Now that you have some perspective on your writing, it is time to revise. First address your critic's comments, which may concern both the style and the substance of the paper. Write another draft that incorporates the suggested changes. Then stand back from your paper and assess it again. Have you addressed your critic's comments fully?

No critic, no matter how generous, will tell you everything you need to know in order to turn your draft into a prize-winning piece of writing. You yourself must take responsibility for revising. One basic strategy of revising is to begin to work on broad revisions to the arguments and narratives, and then work on smaller problems, such as sentences and diction. Finally, you will need to proofread for spelling, grammar, punctuation, and formatting.

Evaluate Your Own Arguments and Narratives

A previous section of this book outlined the key components of historical argumentation. Check your writing thoroughly for the following things: Does the evidence support the inferences? Are all the inferences fully warranted? Does the argument flow and develop in a consistent way? Will readers find this to be an interesting and significant argument?

Chapter Seven of this book outlined the key components of historical narratives. Check your writing to make sure that your audience knows what they need to know in the correct order. Are characters introduced properly? Will your readers find that the chronological sequences of events are in order? Have you included extraneous information that does not drive any of the main stories? Have you established a consistent voice as a narrator?

Evaluate Your Sentences and Word Choices

This book has already given some advice on how to write sentences and how to choose words. While you are revising, you must stand back and look at your sentences as your audience would. Have you chosen strong verbs? Is the order of ideas correct? Do sentences start on common ground and develop a new idea?

Also look at your word choices, or diction, as your audience would. Are you writing in a precise language that your audience will understand? Are you writing in a language they will find incomprehensible or ridiculous?

Proofread the Final Draft

Proofreading is an essential part of writing history. If you sprinkle your writing with minor mistakes, even your most brilliant work will look like a comedy of errors.

Proofreading takes time and patience. Chances are that by the time you start to proofread, you have already revised your paper so many times that your eyes will start to wander. Be disciplined. Print your paper because it is easier to spot mistakes on paper than on the screen. Force yourself to read every word and every line. When this gets too boring, put the writing aside for a short time and come back to it later. You might even try reading the pages in reverse order, so that you focus less on the argument and narrative and more on the proofreading. There is no real way to make proofreading interesting, but still it must be done.

Proofread for Punctuation

Sentences often derive a significant part of their meaning from punctuation, which the following anecdote demonstrates. During a heated debate in Britain's House of Lords, one member insulted another. The insulted lord demanded an apology and the offending lord replied: "I called the Right Honourable Lord a liar it is true and I am sorry for it. And the Right Honourable Lord may punctuate as he pleases."[64]

Imprecise punctuation can indeed cause problems, and these problems are probably more common than you think. You may make mistakes yourself, and you may even notice mistakes in the works of published historians. If you have trouble with punctuation, refer to Turabian or the *Chicago Manual of Style* for guidance. There are plenty of other writing manuals that discuss punctuation, too.

Proofread for Spelling

Spelling errors can be the most embarassing of all mistakes. (Or was that embarrassing?) Everybody should use the spell-checking feature on his or her word-processing program. Just remember that it will not catch all spelling mistakes, especially those involving homonyms. After running the spell-checker, you should print and recheck the paper yourself.

Check Your Formatting

Make sure that you have used a consistent word-processing format throughout the paper. A consistent format is crucial because aberrations are distracting. Your readers will also expect a simple format. Typically, history professors prefer 12-point Times font with one-inch margins and lines double-spaced. Be sure that the pages are numbered, and that your name and the paper's title are on the first page. (Some professors may ask for a title page. Be sure to check with your professor on this and all details of formatting.) While you are checking your format, be sure to print out the paper and check things that do not necessarily appear on the screen when you are writing, such as footnotes, margins, and page numbers.

Read Your Paper Aloud

Reading aloud is the oldest trick for catching writing problems, and it should be the last thing you do before you submit your work. Reading aloud forces you to review every word. Others may think that you are eccentric, but your readers will appreciate the end result: a better piece of writing.

Keep the Rules in Mind, but Enjoy Your Writing

Writing history can be difficult, but most historical writers consider themselves to be quite privileged. Research and writing can be both exhilarating and plodding, but the end result is almost always worth the effort.

◄ Notes ►

1. Peter Novick, *That Noble Dream: The "Objectivity Question" and the American Historical Profession* (Cambridge: Cambridge University Press, 1988), 7.
2. Thucydides, *The Peloponnesian War*, trans. Rex Warner (New York: Penguin Books, 1954; repr. 1984), 145.
3. Paul Kennedy, *The Rise and Fall of the Great Powers: Economic Change and Military Conflict from 1500 to 2000* (New York: Random House, 1987).
4. Arthur J. Ray, *"I Have Lived Here Since the World Began": An Illustrated History of Canadian Native People* (Toronto: Key Porter, 1996).
5. *Canadian History: A Reader's Guide*, M. Brook Taylor and Doug Owram, eds., 2 vols. (Toronto: University of Toronto Press, 1994). Norah Story, *The Oxford Companion to Canadian History and Literature* (Toronto: Oxford University Press, 1967; and the *Supplement to the Oxford Companion to Canadian History and Literature*, ed. William Toye (Toronto: Oxford University Press, 1973). A new edition of the Oxford Companion will be published in 2004. Claude Thibault, *Bibliographia Canadiana* (Don Mills, ON: Longman, Canada: 1973). *Writing About Canada: A Handbook for Modern Canadian History*, ed. John Schultz (Scarborough, ON: Prentice Hall, 1990).
6. *Annual Bulletin of the Historical Association* (UK: Blackwell, for the Historical Association, 1997–present.).
7. Diana Pedersen, *Changing Women, Changing History: A Bibliography of the History of Women in Canada* (Ottawa: Carleton University Press, 1996). George P. Murdock, *The Ethnographic Bibliography of North America*, 4th ed. (New Haven: Human Relations Area Files, 1975); and the *4th edition Supplement 1973–1987* (New Haven: Human Relations Area Files, 1990). Barbara J. Lowther, *A Bibliography of British Columbia: Laying the Foundations, 1849–1899* (Victoria: University of Victoria, 1968). Linda Hale, *The Vancouver Centennial Bibliography* (Vancouver: Vancouver Historical Society, 1986).
8. *The Canadian Encyclopedia* (Edmonton: Hurtig, 1985, 1988 and online at www.thecanadianencyclopedia.com) and *The Canadian Encyclopedia: Year 2000 Edition* (Toronto: McClelland & Stewart, 1999). *The Dictionary of Canadian Biography*, 14 vols. (Toronto: University of Toronto Press and Les Presses de l'Université Laval, 1966–1998). David J. Bercuson and J.L. Granatstein, *The Collins Dictionary of Canadian History, 1867 to the Present* (Don Mills, ON, 1988).
9. R. Cole Harris et al., eds., *The Historical Atlas of Canada*, 3 vols. (Toronto: University of Toronto Press, 1987–1993) and William G. Dean et al. eds., *The Concise Historical Atlas of Canada*, (Toronto: University of Toronto Press, 1998).

10. *The American Historical Association's Guide to Historical Literature*, 3rd ed., ed. Mary Beth Norton and Pamela Gerardi, 2 vols. (New York: Oxford University Press, 1995).

11. Hippocrates, *Precepts*, as quoted by Chester W. Starr in *A History of the Ancient World*, 3rd ed. (New York: Oxford University Press, 1983), 331.

12. For a broader discussion of these research questions, see Richard Marius, *A Short Guide to Writing about History*, 2nd ed. (New York: Harper Collins, 1995), 33–43.

13. Michel-Rolph Trouillot, *Silencing the Past: Power and the Production of History* (Boston: Beacon Press, 1995), 49–53.

14. Loren R. Graham, *The Ghost of the Executed Engineer: Technology and the Fall of the Soviet Union* (Cambridge: Harvard University Press, 1993).

15. Jorge Luis Borges, *Ficciones*, trans. Emecé Editores (New York: Grove Press, 1962), 112, italics added.

16. Cicero, *Pro Publio Sestio*, 2.62. As quoted by John Bartlett and Justin Kaplan, eds., *Bartlett's Familiar Quotations*, 16th ed. (Boston: Little Brown, 1992), 87.

17. These suggestions are taken from Gordon Harvey, *Writing with Sources* (Cambridge: Harvard University, 1995), 27–9.

18. Joyce Lee Malcolm, *To Keep and Bear Arms: The Origins of an Anglo-American Right* (Cambridge: Harvard University Press, 1994), 143.

19. Jack P. Greene, *Pursuits of Happiness: The Social Development of Early Modern British Colonies and the Formation of American Culture* (Chapel Hill: University of North Carolina Press, 1988), 61.

20. E.P. Thompson, *The Making of the English Working Class* (New York: Vintage Books, 1963; pbk. ed. 1966), 193–4.

21. "'The Declaration of the Reformers of the City of Toronto to their Fellow-Reformers in Upper Canada, Toronto, August 2, 1837,' *The Constitution*," in Colin Read and Ronald J. Stagg, eds., *The Rebellion of 1837 in Upper Canada: A Collection of Documents* (Ottawa: Carleton University Press, 1985), 60.

22. Walter MacDougall, *The Heavens and the Earth: A Political History of the Space Age* (New York: Basic Books, 1985), 8.

23. MacDougall, *Heavens and Earth*, 8.

24. Harvey, *Writing with Sources*, 21–3.

25. Colin M. Coates, "Commemorating the Woman Warrior of New France, Madeleine de Verchères, 1696–1930," in *Gender and History in Canada*, ed. Joy Parr and Mark Rosenfeld (Toronto: Copp Clark, 1996), 130.

26. Harvey, *Writing with Sources*, 13–16.

27. Walt Whitman, "The Real War Will Never Get in the Books," *Specimen Days* (New York: Signet Classic, 1961), 112.

28. Deborah E. Lipstadt, *Denying the Holocaust* (New York: Penguin, 1993).

29. Philip D. Curtin, *The Atlantic Slave Trade: A Census* (Madison: University of Wisconsin Press, 1969).

30. Prasenjit Duara, *Culture, Power, and the State: Rural North China, 1900–1942* (Stanford: Stanford University Press, 1988). Philip C. C. Huang, *The Peasant Economy and Social Change in North China* (Stanford: Stanford University Press, 1985). Ramon Myers, *The Chinese Peasant Economy: Agricultural Development in Hopei and Shantung, 1840–1940* (Cambridge: Harvard University Press, 1970).

31. Gerald L. Geison, *The Private Science of Louis Pasteur* (Princeton: Princeton University Press, 1995), 149–56.

32. James Fairhead and Melissa Leach, *Misreading the African Landscape: Society and Ecology in a Forest-Savanna Mosaic* (Cambridge: Cambridge University Press, 1996).

33. Jan Vansina, *Living with Africa* (Madison: University of Wisconsin Press, 1994), 16–17.

34. Pete Daniel, *Standing at the Crossroads: Southern Life in the Twentieth Century* (Baltimore: The Johns Hopkins University Press, 1986; 2nd ed. 1996), 21–22.

35. James C. Cobb, *The Most Southern Place on Earth: The Mississippi Delta and the Roots of Regional Identity* (New York: Oxford University Press, 1992), 290.

36. Margaret Washington Creel, "Gullah Attitudes toward Life and Death," and Robert Farris Thompson, "Kongo Influences on African-American Artistic Culture," in *Africanisms in American Culture*, ed. Joseph E. Holloway (Bloomington: Indiana University Press, 1990), 81–2, 154.

37. John Janzen and Wyatt MacGaffey, *An Anthology of Kongo Religion: Primary Texts from Lower Zaïre* (Lawrence: University of Kansas, 1974), 73–5.

38. Jules David Prown, "Mind in Matter: An Introduction to Material Culture Theory and Method," in *Material Life in America, 1600–1860*, ed. Robert Blair St. George (Boston: Northeastern University Press, 1991), 17–35. Thanks to Elizabeth Abrams for suggesting this article.

39. Charles S. Maier, *The Unmasterable Past: History, Holocaust, and German National Identity* (Cambridge: Harvard University Press, 1988), 1.

40. Georges Lefebvre, *The Coming of the French Revolution*, trans. R.R. Palmer (Princeton: Princeton University Press, 1947; rev. ed. 1989).

41. Betty Jo Teeter Dobbs, *The Janus Face of Genius: The Role of Alchemy in Newton's Thought* (Cambridge: Cambridge University Press, 1991).

42. Samuel Eliot Morison, "History as a Literary Art: An Appeal to Young Historians," *Old South Leaflets* ser. 2, no. 1 (Boston: Old South Association, 1946): 7.

43. Caroline Walker Bynum, *Holy Feast and Holy Fast: The Religious Significance of Food to Medieval Women* (Berkeley and Los Angeles: University of California Press, 1987), 1.

44. Michel F. Girard, "The Oka Crisis from an Environmental History Perspective, 1870-1990," in *Readings in Canadian History: Post-Confederation*, 4th ed., ed. R. Douglas Francis and Donald B. Smith (Toronto: Harcourt Brace, 1994), 578–9. Girard's citations have not been included in this citation.

45. Daniel Headrick, *The Tools of Empire: Technology and European Imperialism in the Nineteenth Century* (Oxford: Oxford University Press, 1981), 85–6.

46. A. I. Sabra, "Situating Arabic Science: Locality versus Essence," the History of Science Society Distinguished Lecture, published in *Isis* 87, no. 4 (December 1996): 654–70. Quotation from p. 668.

47. William Cronon, *Changes in the Land: Indians, Colonists, and the Ecology of New England* (New York: Hill and Wang, 1983), 6.

48. Carl Degler, *In Search of Human Nature: The Decline and Revival of Darwinism in American Social Thought* (Oxford: Oxford University Press, 1991), vii.

49. Robert Jay Lifton, *The Nazi Doctors: Killing and the Psychology of Genocide* (New York: Basic Books, 1986), 341, 378.

50. William Sheridan Allen, *The Nazi Seizure of Power: The Experience of a Single German Town, 1922–1945* (New York: Franklin Watts, 1965; rev. ed. 1984), 207.

51. Robert S. McElvaine, *Eve's Seed: Biology, the Sexes, and the Course of History* (New York: McGraw-Hill, 2001), 26–32.

52. Veronica Strong-Boag, "Home Dreams: Women and the Suburban Experiment in Canada, 1945–1960," *Readings in Canadian History: Post-Confederation*, 4th ed., ed. R. Douglas Francis and Donald B. Smith (Toronto: Harcourt Brace, 1994), 503.

53. Herodotus, *The Histories*, trans. Aubrey de Sélincourt (New York: Penguin Classics, 1954; rev. ed. 1983), 519.

54. Starr, *History of the Ancient World*, 294–5.

55. Franklin W. Knight, *The Caribbean: The Genesis of a Fragmented Nationalism*, 2nd ed. (New York: Oxford University Press, 1990).

56. Christopher Hibbert, *The Great Mutiny: India 1857* (New York: Penguin Books, 1978), 63.

57. John Demos, *The Unredeemed Captive: A Family Story from Early America* (New York: Vintage Books, 1994), 146.

58. Hibbert, *Great Mutiny*, 24.

59. Hibbert, *Great Mutiny*, 388.

60. Winston S. Churchill, *The Birth of Britain*, vol. 1 in *History of the English Speaking Peoples* (New York: Dodd, Mead, and Co., 1956; Bantam, 1974), 131.

61. *Bartlett's Familiar Quotations*, 16th ed., p. 620.

62. James Belich, *The Victorian Interpretation of Racial Conflict: The Maori, the British, and the New Zealand Wars* (Montreal and Kingston: McGill-Queen's University Press, 1989), 20–1.

63. George Orwell, "Politics and the English Language," in *Fields of Writing*, eds. Nancy Comley et al., 4th ed. (New York: St. Martin's Press, 1994), 618.

64. Mary Refling et al., Postings to the H-Albion bulletin board, 8–10 July 1997 <http://h-net2.msu.edu/~albion>.

⊰ Index ⊱